THE END OF MY LIFE IS KILLING ME

Praise for

The End of My Life Is Killing Me

"Laugh-out-loud hilarious about the things we're all terrified to say. Every chapter is a reminder that life is a tragicomedy, and we can curl up in a ball and hide under the covers or better yet, we can curl up with this brilliant book."

—MOLLY JONG-FAST, author of *How to Lose Your Mother*

"You will fall in love with Annabelle Gurwitch's smart, affirming, funny, and wise approach to embracing life fully. A delight to read that will also leave you deeply moved."

—SUSAN ORLEAN, author of *The Library Book*

"Resilient, hilarious, unfiltered, and honest, just like the author herself. Great writing . . . that feels like a friend. Adversity's greatest foe is her singular wit."

—STEVEN ROWLEY, author of *The Guncle*

"*The End of My Life is Killing Me* has wit sharp enough to cut through sentimentality and honesty that refuses to look away. Part memoir, part laugh-out-loud commentary on the absurd and irritating realities of life and death, it's a reminder that even in our darkest hours, we can choose what to notice, what to celebrate, and how to live."

—GRETCHEN RUBIN, author of *The Happiness Project*

"Reading Annabelle Gurwitch's extraordinary new book is like spending time over a glass (or two) of wine with your funniest, smartest, wisest friend as she drops powerful and irreverent truth bombs about all the things that matter most and least. It's a Trojan Horse of sorts: a hysterically funny page-turner that is packed throughout with practical advice and timeless wisdom."

—WILL SCHWALBE, author of *The End of Your Life Book Club*

"Gurwitch is at her most fearless—witty, skeptical, and wide awake to the absurdities of being alive. With her singular blend of humor and insight, Gurwitch reminds us that even in life's most unexpected and uncertain moments, choosing what to pay attention to, who matters, and how you want to live each day is its own form of hope."

—LORI GOTTLIEB, author of *Maybe You Should Talk to Someone*

"We don't tend to think of cancer narratives as hilarious, and we don't tend to think of humor as helpful, but I promise you, this book is both. On the page, Gurwitch is a wisecracking, unflinching, insightful heroine and like your best friend who you never want to get off the phone with."

—SARAH RUHL, author of *Smile: The Story of a Face*

"Gurwitch trains her masterful blend of humor, insight, and pointed social and political critique on her own experience with cancer. The result is one of the most generous books I've ever read. Gurwitch lights the way for anyone who wants to know how to live, against any odds, filled with passion, a sense of adventure, and kindness."

—MARISA SILVER, author of *Mary Coin*

"With this hilarious and poignant book, the great Annabelle Gurwitch proves that inspirational literature can be spiky and fun and prone to sentences like 'Juicers are the Waterford crystal bowls for the newly diagnosed.' What doesn't kill her makes her funnier. All hail!"

—HENRY ALFORD, author of *I Dream of Joni*

Previous Praise

"Annabelle Gurwitch is sharp-eyed, unfoolable, and hilarious. The only downside of this book is that it's bound to deepen your laugh lines."

—BARBARA EHRENREICH, author of *Nickel and Dimed*

"A pure delight, full of ambivalence, regret, laughter, rage, melancholy, and honest observations about grappling with life's bewildering cavalcade of surprises and disappointments."

—HEATHER HAVRILESKY, author of *What If This Were Enough?*

"Reading Annabelle Gurwitch feels like staying up all night in a freewheeling conversation with my funniest, wisest, most magnetic friend."

—MARIA SEMPLE, author of *Where'd You Go, Bernadette?*

"Gurwitch mines our generational ill luck for humor and insight as only a resilient latchkey kid can: with an arched brow and a gimlet eye."

—ADA CALHOUN, author of *Why We Can't Sleep*

"Gurwitch has an amazing—and very welcome—knack for wringing humor from pathos and locating sublimity in absurdity. A breezily hilarious but deeply affecting exploration of loss, human connection, and mortality."

—CARINA CHOCANO, author of *You Play the Girl*

"Gurwitch manages to find humor in setbacks. Ultimately, this is a story about harnessing resilience and learning how life's disappointments can teach you about the things that matter most."

—*The New York Times*

"Droll, self-deprecating Gurwitch is very funny—like Rhoda Morgenstern on *The Mary Tyler Moore Show*, but delivering not so much one-liners or gags as stories that shift life's viewfinder."

—*The National Book Review*

"Gurwitch succeeds by evoking emotions that cut to the core of our humanity, and giving us laughs along the way."

—*Los Angeles Review of Books*

"[Gurwitch] trains a skeptical eye on her era's foibles in the manner of a Dorothy Parker, leavens it with the hausfrau élan of an Erma Bombeck, and spices it with her own witty, irrepressible personality."

—*Charleston Post and Courier*

"Her stories are as personal as they are universal . . . Gurwitch will have readers rolling with laughter one minute and picking up the phone to commiserate with friends or family the next."

—*Library Journal*

Also by Annabelle Gurwitch

You're Leaving When?
adventures in downward mobility

Wherever You Go, There They Are
stories about my family you might relate to

I See You Made an Effort
compliments, indignities and survival stories from the edge of 50

Fired!
tales of the canned, canceled, downsized, and dismissed

By Annabelle Gurwitch and Jeff Kahn

You Say Tomato, I Say Shut Up
a love story

THE END OF MY LIFE IS KILLING ME

THE UNEXPECTED JOYS OF A CANCER SLACKER

ANNABELLE GURWITCH

Zibby Publishing
New York

The End of My Life Is Killing Me
the unexpected joys of a cancer slacker

Copyright © 2026 by Annabelle Gurwitch

All rights reserved. No part of this book may be used, reproduced, distributed, or transmitted in any form or by any means without the prior written permission of the publisher, except as permitted by U.S. copyright law. Published in the United States by Zibby Publishing, New York.

ZIBBY, Zibby Publishing, colophon, and associated logos are trademarks and/or registered trademarks of Zibby Media LLC.

The author has tried to re-create events, locales, and conversations based on their own memories and those of others. In some instances, in order to maintain their anonymity, certain names, characteristics, and locations have been changed.

Some of these essays previously appeared, in slightly different form, in the following publications: *The New York Times* ("The Coronavirus Saved My Life" and "The End of My Life Is Killing Me") and *The Washington Post* ("The Happiest Sea Sponge in the Ocean" and "The Wall of No").

"We're Gonna Die" © Young Jean Lee (Lincoln Center production, LCT3, 2021)

"The Humanoid Stain" © Barbara Ehrenreich (*Baffler* Magazine, 2019)

Library of Congress Control Number: 2025946336
Hardcover ISBN: 978-1-968506-06-3
Paperback ISBN: 979-8-9923770-7-1
eBook ISBN: 979-8-9923770-8-8

Book Design by Westchester Publishing Services
Cover Design by Graça Tito
Cover Art © Lucia Heffernan

www.zibbymedia.com

Printed in the United States of America

10 9 8 7 6 5 4 3 2

for science,
you had me at suspicious mass

If the drink is bitter, turn yourself to wine.
—Rainer Maria Rilke

Table of Contents

That Was Then, Bread Is Now (an Introduction)

It was a few months after my out-of-the-blue diagnosis with stage 4 lung cancer when I was reunited with one of the comforts of my childhood: bread. I was on my daily walk when I found myself hypnotized by the wall of breads in my local French bakery, drawn in by the yeasty scent. Olive, raisin and walnut, sesame, and rustic country white loaves cozily stacked in kindergarten cubby–like wooden shelving. Some lizard-brain response kicked in, and the next thing I knew, I was racing home with a baguette. I pressed on the paper bag repeatedly, my pace increasing with anticipation. The crust had *give* to it, just like my preferred pillow, a Tempur-Pedic, with its supportive hard shell and cushy inside. I needed to eat a pillow!

Prior to that day, bread hadn't passed my lips for decades. I'd rigorously maintained a svelte figure because, above all, I'm practical, a habit I picked up as a cash-strapped young actress subsisting on a diet of big dreams and day-old bodega salad bar fare. I came of age at a time when women were encouraged to build wardrobes around investment pieces; I'd done that in my thirties and forties and was still trying to squeeze into them. Mind you, I've never given up chocolate: I'm vain but I'm not crazy; I keep emergency chocolate in my earthquake kit.

I'd barely crossed the threshold when I tore into it. The fluffy middle was my Proustian madeleine, bringing back memories of a toasted sesame bagel with wasabi-infused cream cheese that I'd had years earlier, while on a book tour, at Zingerman's Bakehouse in Ann Arbor, Michigan. I spent close to an hour licking the spread like an ice-cream cone, savoring the pairing of cool dairy creaminess and earthy warm horseradish. Then, after working my way through half of the bagel, I carefully wrapped up the other half to save for the next day's breakfast. When I revisit that memory, it's laughable—and a little hashtag sad—because that kind of parsimonious meting out of pleasure was emblematic of how I lived in the *before days.*

The stories in this book chronicle my attempts, successful and otherwise, to rekindle my joie de vivre in the *after days*, the five years since being diagnosed with a disease with a "poor outcome." That's medical-establishment speak for an incurable malady, which is a euphemism for a terminal illness, which is a nicer way of saying: No one gets out of here alive. A cure for what I have will be found, but will that happen in time for me? Fingers crossed. An oncologist introducing me before I spoke at the International Association for the Study of Lung Cancer (IASLC) World Conference in 2024 characterized me as "a ticking time bomb." I politely corrected him. "I'm a very fashionable ticking time bomb."

Stories like mine typically portray a before and after existence. Before the diagnosis, my life was like this . . . After the diagnosis, like that . . . Many of these stories involve the chronicling of a debilitating medical odyssey. This isn't that. Through the miracle of modern science—not to mention the good fortune of having access to therapies that are unavailable to many around the globe and even in the contiguous United States—and dumb luck, I was granted a temporary reprieve.

Since my diagnosis in 2020, my physical health has been held stable with a one-pill, once-a-day medication. The drug I take is one of a class of targeted therapies that are changing the paradigm of medicine, allowing for terminal diseases to be managed like chronic illnesses. But with the kind of lung cancer I have, the medication eventually stops working. The disease is as wily as a toddler, it figures out a work-around to any kind of containment. The cancer will thwart the medication and spread, and I will have to move to one or more grueling regimens, i.e., chemotherapy and radiation. Timeline unknown. The science is improving at an astonishing pace. In fact, I was at the world lung cancer conference in Barcelona in September 2025, where promising trial results were shared involving antibody-drug conjugates (ADCs), a new, smarter form of chemotherapy, which could extend my time with less toxicities. But even those measures don't offer a cure. I was asymptomatic when diagnosed, and there's a great likelihood that I won't have the benefit of worsening symptoms to alert me when the medication stops working. This adds to the cognitive dissonance of looking and feeling essentially unchanged even though my life has been irreversibly altered.

My prognosis left my emotional well-being in ruins.

Living with this kind of precariousness produces the sort of debilitating dread described by Mexican philosopher Emilio Uranga as "existential wobbliness." Uranga characterized this kind of vacillating between anxiety and deep gloom as *zozobra*, a Spanish word that translates to shipwrecked. "A shipwreck of the soul," he called it. Exactly. I don't believe in a soul but my nonexistent soul felt shipwrecked. Uranga wrote that in this fraught condition, decision-making becomes unfathomable and "the soul suffers, it feels torn and wounded." At the same time, I have entertained fleeting but troublingly reassuring fantasies of a quick and (hopefully) painless demise, sparing my family the financial cost of a slow decline and myself a fate more unbearable than my own exit from this world: my child dying before me. This existential relief felt shameful to even acknowledge. "You're in the bardo," my friend Tonya said. Tibetan Buddhism loosely defines a bardo as an intermediate space between life and death. But since I've got only a first-three-pages-of-every-book-about-Buddhism understanding of such things, I just call this chapter *my* after life, but which is thankfully not *the afterlife.*

Bread helped. That first baguette was the gateway bread to a new lease on life. Bread answered a need, but it wasn't *the* answer.

When you get diagnosed with cancer, a tsunami of decisions descends upon you: Where should you receive treatment, which assets or organs might you sell to afford your care, but perhaps, most important, what's your cancer persona? There are cancer thrivers, cancer survivors, crazy sexy cancers, and cancer vixens, but I didn't want to adopt a performative indefatigability or accomplish heroic feats that would turn me into someone's idea of a cancer warrior. I vowed to be an underachiever. A cancer slacker. I was already in a competitive business: Did I have to win at cancer too? I needed to carve out an identity that would mean the cancer wouldn't define me, or, as my friend Leslie called it, turn me into *Annabelle Cancer.*

To do things differently seemed important. That meant thinking radically differently. In the past few years, the word *radical* has become *radically* oversubscribed. Radical acceptance, radical compassion, I'm certain someone in my zip code offers a workshop in radical Swiffering, but summoning a radical curiosity in my *after life* seemed crucial because what I wanted most was to curl up into the fetal position and stay there indefinitely.

So I did the opposite of what my instincts were telling me. I took contrary action. Mostly. I have a slide-y commitment to follow-through and bristle at adopting life philosophies that require strict adherence and fealty—that kind of thinking can lead to authoritarian creep, adoption of the Paleo diet, the use of the phrase "it's all good," and bangs. I had only one criterion if there was such a thing: I would make choices that sent me outside my comfort zone.

I'm also constitutionally incapable of embracing popular trends. I'd like to coin a word for "and they gave in to birding as people tend to do, having suffered a trauma or when nearing the end of life." According to the U.S. Fish and Wildlife Service, one third of Americans took up birdwatching during Covid. I didn't become a birder, although I am now heavily invested in the continued happiness of Jackie and Shadow, the bald eagles of Big Bear. The couple's nest atop a towering Jeffrey pine has a live webcam feed that can be viewed on YouTube. When Jackie's eggs failed to hatch in 2023, I cried my eyes out for days.

I wasn't committing to an exact binary; that would be a strategy doomed to failure. This is where radical curiosity comes in. I said yes to test-driving the concept of calm as a form of resistance when panic seemed more appropriate. Or shifting my attention to that exquisite layer of beauty that lies just beneath the ordinary, what French author Georges Perec called "the infra-ordinary." In his 1973 essay "Approaches to What?" Perec proposed that as a society we'd become too focused on the extraordinary. "We sleep through our lives in a dreamless sleep. But where is our life? Where is our body? Where is our space?" To wake up, we'd need to venture from our habitual ways of seeing the world. To "defamiliarize the familiar." The essay was published over half a century ago. What would he say if he were alive now?

I'd internalized the call to seize the day and live each day as if it's your last, but I discovered that you can carpe too much diem. In fact, older translations of *carpe* imply something kinder, gentler, *pluck*. So, the phrase carpe diem is a prompt to pluck the day, an idea that appealed to me.

And so, I've come to find myself in unlikely places, like selling merch for a heavy metal band on a van tour around Europe and communing with an angel. My biggest adventures were imperceptible to the eye, like when you buy a house and you want to add a wet room with a freestanding bathtub, but what really matters is the infrastructure. Foundationally transformative gestures like expressing love or forgiveness became essential to my survival.

I took inspiration from Henri Matisse. Matisse was seventy-one when he suffered a life-threatening illness. Surprised by his own survival, he returned to his studio, abandoned his Fauvist roots, and began the work he referred to as "cutouts." Painted-on paper that was then cut and pasted onto canvases, the "Blue Nudes" series are some of the most well-known of that genre. Matisse dubbed this reinvigorated self his "second life."

"Only what I created after my illness constitutes my real self: free, liberated," he was quoted as saying. I took only one semester of art history, so who am I to argue with Matisse, but I love those early works. His zest to evolve beyond the known self, at seventy-one, seemed to portend that immutable attributes might be less fixed than I'd assumed. There's a tendency for folks who are granted extra time on their dance card to undervalue their *before times. It was only after surviving X, I really learned how to live.* Except for all the breads I missed out on, I had a pretty decent first life. I prefer to describe the adaptations I have made with the sage words of Ashley, my yoga teacher: "You're perfect as you are, and you could use a little improvement."

As for my favorite outfits? Well, they are a bit snugger now, but eventually, the cancer will take care of that. Cancer humor, like cancer, will test your patience.

When I was an actress, I carried a small dispenser of Rescue Remedy in my purse. Before auditions, I'd place the homeopathic pastilles under my tongue to tame my nerves. I can't guarantee that the rescues I explore in this book will provide relief if you are experiencing your own shipwreck of the soul, but I can vouch that they are more potent than sucking on lavender-flavored sugar drops. My hope is that this book offers a bit of comfort, community, laughter, and an invitation to curiosity. Fingers crossed.

The Coronavirus Saved My Life

The ten-mile stretch of the California State Route 2 that connects the greater Los Angeles Basin to Pasadena is a lost highway. A bardo. A no-man's-land. There are sections of Route 2 that treat you to spectacular and breathtaking mountain scenery, but no one has bothered to landscape the bleak concrete artery. Like in *Saturday Night Live*'s "The Californians," I'd taken the 5 to the 134 to the 210 to the 2, an improbable number of connections to reach a destination located just a few miles from my home. There are moments when you can no longer see the city you've come from nor the one you're headed toward. Proof of Gertrude Stein's quip that in California "there's no *there* there."

It was the start of summer, June 2020. My son, Ezra, had just finished college on the East Coast. Instead of attending the graduation ceremony in person, parents were invited to tune in to a speech by the dean on a Zoom rife with technical difficulties. The event sputtered to a close with an alphabetized list of the students' names scrolling by on a black screen. Even the font was unremarkable.

Ezra returned home to a Los Angeles in lockdown. We planned to strictly follow the recommended protocols, including a quarantine before cohabitating. Ezra would hunker down in the guest bedroom while I had the run of the house. But in a turn of events that no parent will find surprising, I got stuck with the guest room, dashing to the kitchen for the occasional snack. This was during the anxious period before home-testing kits came on the market and people were microwaving their mail, grocery shopping in homemade hazmat suits, and stockpiling hand sanitizer.

On day fourteen, we double-masked it and hopped into the car with windows wide open to a drive-through testing station at Dodger Stadium. A line of cars snaked around the perimeter. The wait threatened to last several hours, longer than I had patience for after two weeks in the eight-by-ten-foot guest bedroom.

We rerouted to a random urgent care in Eagle Rock, a sleepy suburb just north of Los Angeles, on the recommendation of Emily, a writer friend whose local mom LISTSERV always came through. The sparsely staffed storefront facility was located in a mini-mall, sandwiched between an Olive Garden and an Ulta Beauty, both shuttered.

In the parking lot, we filled out questionnaires asking if we had Covid symptoms. I mentioned having a little cough. We tested, got the all-clear, but the doctor suggested I have a chest X-ray "just to be sure." Who gets an X-ray at an urgent care unless they've broken a limb? I was sure this was the equivalent of a cosmetic counter upsell. You walk in for a mascara and walk out with a pricey night cream.

"It's really no big deal," I said. But the doctor was persistent and kind of adorable. He looked to be in his early forties, had twinkly eyes, a chaotic tousle of hair, and a warm way with words. Maybe he had a thing for older women?

"You're fine," he said when he returned fifteen minutes later with my results.

We were speeding home on that desolate stretch when we heard the front fender of my car scraping the pavement. I'd caught it on something weeks earlier and jerry-rigged it in place with duct tape. Now it had broken loose. I pulled off on the shoulder, inched toward the off-ramp, and parked in front of a boarded-up auto repair shop.

The morning air was crisp, the cloudless sky uncommonly clear. One bright spot during the pandemic was that the dearth of traffic meant pollution levels fell precipitously. There was an eerie calm, like the moments just before the first zombie attack.

I love zombie movies. The genre offers a wellspring of catastrophes: vigilante justice gone amok, alien invasions, cli-fi (climate science fiction, which tends to be ripped from the headlines and hits a little too close to home). A zombie apocalypse offers my kind of dystopian merriment because it's never going to happen. I do a pretty good zombie walk: slouchy trudge, vacant gaze, slack jaw. I'd hoped to get cast as the walking dead back in my acting days. Another of my useless skills that I'd trot out when Ezra annoyed me as a kid. I'd recruited him into my love of the genre—we'd even done zombie escape rooms together.

"This is just like a zombie movie," I said when AAA didn't answer.

"Mom!" Erza groaned.

I left a message for roadside assistance, and a few minutes later my phone rang. It wasn't AAA. It was the adorable urgent care doc.

"Is your son with you?" he asked.

Yep, he was calling to ask me out.

"Would you prefer to talk privately?" he continued.

With a smug "still got it" grin, I assured Eagle Rock's Dr. McDreamy it was fine to talk on speakerphone.

"I'm so sorry," he said. "I made a mistake. I read you the wrong results. You have a concerning mass on your right lung."

Ezra looked stricken.

In the periphery of my vision, I could see his jaw drop open. Much later, he would say that he knew that this was that life-changing phone call, in that way that makes you question the possibility of prescience, even as you know that this kind of feeling is unreliable.

"Thanks, I've got a doctor and I'll get right on that," I chirped, as if I was hopping off the phone to check on that brisket roasting in the oven.

There's that saying, "When the going gets tough, the tough get going." For me, it's more like, "When the going gets tough, the tough get chatty." Any emotional reaction I might have had to Dr. McDreamy insisting I return for more tests was hampered by my reflexive protect-the-kid mode. "I'm sure it's nothing," I repeatedly said to Ezra, a nervous incantation, while we waited for an Uber. "Can you imagine the other person who got the call that they had a concerning mass on their lung? I hope they didn't jump out of a window."

This was the worst thing to say, but I wasn't thinking, I was talking.

Ezra said little, because how could he? I was doing all the talking. An Uber drove us home. The next day I got the car towed.

That was the start of my *after life*. I just didn't know it.

When my new BFF, a pulmonologist, entered my life, his first question before "How are you feeling?" was "Do you have a good insurance plan?"

"I think so?"

"Good. Don't make any changes."

I wouldn't understand the implications of that question until many months later.

We quickly fell into an Abbott and Costello "Who's on First?" routine as we set out to prove whatever was going on in my lungs wasn't cancer.

"Valley fever," I suggested, because it sounded vaguely festive, like something Moon Unit Zappa sang about in the 1980s that was endemic to the San Fernando Valley—where I'd logged countless hours on the sets of television shows. It was a consequential but treatable condition in which dust particles get lodged in the lungs.

The pulmonologist suspected lipoid pneumonia, another garden-variety but treatable condition.

"Have you been ingesting castor oil?" he asked. During the early part of the twentieth century, castor oil was a common household remedy and a staple in every American pantry. How ancient did this doctor think I was? But then, I noticed that castor oil was listed just after H_2O as the primary ingredient of a French facial mist I'd been spritzing my face with several times a day since the start of the pandemic. This elixir contained extracts of orange blossoms, lavender, myrrh, and grapevines. Dousing myself transported me to the lavender fields of the French Cosmetic Valley. The Cosmetic Valley is located in the Chartres region of France and is home to numerous skin-care laboratories, where I'd hoped to convince some media outlet to send me on assignment one day. Wouldn't it be just like me to have given myself some kind of health condition in the name of vanity?

For the next two months, I ping-ponged between imaging centers for X-rays, IV contrast scans, oral contrast scans, scans that made you feel like you'd peed your pants, scans that bonged like a bad club remix. I approached this investigation like a medical mystery scavenger hunt, greeting technicians with a smile and a spring in my step, as if energy alone was prophylactic.

I'd treated the pandemic like boot camp: hiking daily, eating low on the food chain. I'd been in good health, but felt even better than I had in years. Against the backdrop of Covid, my condition seemed superfluous. People were checking into hospitals and not checking out.

Ezra, like so many 2020 graduates, was adjusting to the life every twentysomething dreams of: stuck at home, in their childhood bedroom. Worried over his obvious distress, I shared the bare minimum of information. For the most part, I avoided him. The only activity we did together was make lunch. Every Sunday morning for six months, we woke early, shopped, and assembled ten or so meals, then dropped them off at a local distribution site for neighbors struggling to feed their families. I was desperate to provide purpose to our blobby pandemic days, now made more diffuse by my uncertain health.

"Do you think you have cancer? You know your body best," my friend Tonya said when I told her about the testing.

Did I? Does anyone? Outside of that pesky cough, I'd been asymptomatic. I'd never known anyone to have a serious illness without some sign of trouble.

"No news is good news," others repeated.

"Isn't no news just no news?" I'd asked.

The appointments had their own surreal peculiarity. I was going it alone, adding to the unreality of it all. Masking was mandatory with Covid surging, so I was unable to read the facial expressions of the doctors, nurses, or technicians on whom I was suddenly dependent. They'd never seen my unmasked face either. Each time I encountered a new practitioner, I'd pull out my cell phone. "This is me and my kid," I'd say, showing off my screen saver, a photo of us from happier times.

After three months of scans proved inconclusive, a surgical biopsy was scheduled. As I was wheeled into the operating theater, I flashed on another dystopian movie genre: the transhumanism, organ-harvesting plot. I asked the doctor to show me her face to make sure it matched the picture on her ID.

I was so anxious about getting the results from Dr. Abbott and Costello that I asked my friend Juel to drive me to the appointment. Our boys had been childhood friends and college roommates. In her lengthy career as a casting director, she had worked with some of the most exacting creatives in the business and never lost her cool. My cousin Ruth worked in the hospital's administration, and I wrangled permission for her to accompany me.

The biopsy concretized a verdict: malignant adenocarcinoma.

Dr. Abbott and Costello referred me to an oncologist.

"So . . . does this have a stage?" I asked.

This wasn't my first rodeo. I'd accompanied friends and family members to these types of appointments.

"The oncologist will answer any questions you have."

"But I want to keep seeing you," I said, like a five-year-old who'd just been told they were too old to visit Santa.

Afterward, Ruth walked me to Juel's car.

"The doctor says it's adenocarcinoma," Ruth said to her.

"It's cancer. It's in my lungs. I have lung cancer," I said, still in shock.

"He didn't use the words *lung cancer*," Ruth insisted.

Juel and I argued this point over the ride home.

"I have lung cancer."

"He didn't say that."

"But that's what that means. Lung cancer!"

"Stop saying that!"

"Lung cancer!"

My entire life was turning into a comedy routine.

I thought I'd been around long enough to know the good cancers from the bad ones, but lung cancer wasn't even on my radar. The only information I had came from Dr. Google. "Annabelle, it's bad," my keep-on-the-sunny-side-of-life hiking buddy, Rose, said. She'd appointed herself my researcher. Later, I would learn that unless you're doing very directed searches, you're going to get dangerously out-of-date information and you're better off bingeing funny cat videos.

While I braced myself for whatever was coming next, swimming was my solace. I alternated between neighbors' pools. My world had gotten so small. My house, the single remaining continent. Sally's pool, with its cobalt blue tiles, was plunging into the deep California Pacific; John and Randy's, with its 1950s corrugated fiberglass cover casting a mossy hue, wading in the shallow Atlantic off the coast of South Florida. These were felt associations, unscientific and uncomplicated by factual verification and therefore reassuring. I grew up in cities on coastlines, so water is a second skin. In actuality, Sally's house was eastward and John's westward, but the world was backward, so why shouldn't geography be flipped too?

Floating, suspended in water, I could suspend my disbelief. Gliding across the surface, then diving down, holding my breath to swim the length of the pool, I'd emerge heaving. The exertion was exhilarating. Empowering. It seemed confirmation that all would be okay, after all.

A week later, I blow-dried my hair for the first time since the start of the pandemic, put on makeup and a cheery pussy-bow blouse, picked wildflowers from my garden, and strategically positioned them for maximum visibility in the Zoom frame for my telehealth appointment with the oncologist.

"We all get dressed up for appointments because we want the doctors to think we're worth saving," Jill Feldman, cofounder of a lung cancer support group, confirmed three years later at a conference for the study of lung cancer in Singapore, an event I never imagined attending.

It was during the telehealth Zoom that the words "lung cancer" and "stage four" were first spoken.

"Stage four?"

"We'll do the best we can, for as long as we can," the oncologist said, eyes downcast, like he was poised to shovel dirt onto my coffin.

"How is that possible?" I'd gone from a concerning mass to deathly ill? The high-res scans showed not just one, but numerous tumors and "ground-glass opacities," hazy cancerous areas spanning both lungs.

"You've probably had this for years," the oncologist explained as I sobbed. Because I'd never had a baseline scan, we didn't know if the cancer was slow-growing or aggressive.

"What about surgery?" I asked.

"God, no. You have too much diseased tissue. You need to have some lung left."

"Well, what's stage five?" I asked, momentarily forgetting that stage 5 is death.

Tissue from my biopsy was sent to a specialized lab to identify the specific type of lung cancer I had. There were different types of lung cancer? Who knew? This would determine the kind of "we'll do the best we can" treatment regimen we'd institute on the way to my inevitable "for as long as we can" exit, "pursued by a bear."

That's Shakespeare's stage direction for meeting an untimely and dramatic demise.

Cari, a friend and non-Hodgkin's lymphoma survivor, was sitting in on my call. Seeing my shock after the diagnosis, she asked if I could take something for anxiety.

"Klonopin?" she offered.

"No," he replied. "That can lead to addiction."

"What about an occasional glass of wine?"

"Half a glass," he replied.

When the Zoom ended, Cari dubbed the oncologist Dr. Sad Eyes, based on both affect and appearance. The nickname stuck.

Although telehealth has been a game changer in bridging inequities in health care by providing access in hard-to-reach corners of the globe, I will always feel it gave me cancer.

I cried until the sun set. As though under the cover of darkness, I called my sister and closest friends, still seated in front of my flower arrangement. I shared what I knew, which wasn't much. My life would never be the same, but a trace of me remained intact. There's that old question: Would you rather be happy or right? Right, of course.

My final call was to Juel. "Guess who was right? I have lung cancer. I win!"

Given the absence of symptoms, the stage 4 diagnosis was like a sucker punch. If I could be so wrong about the state of my health, how could I trust anything? The skills I'd amassed over a lifetime had been raptured seemingly overnight, leaving panic, worry, and indecision behind. I lost confidence in my ability to string words together. I was speaking too slowly, like a record playing at the wrong speed. Composing a single sentence required herculean effort, so writing assignments went on indefinite hold. I lost all certainty in my body's reliability. I held on to walls while walking, unsure if my legs would give out without warning.

The most shattering of all the losses was my ability to navigate the world. After my first year of college, my family suffered a financial wipeout. I'd dropped out of NYU, stayed on in the city, and somehow made my way. Scrappiness and self-reliance became second nature.

"There are many ways to get to the same destination," I told Ezra repeatedly. This was not only a practical skill, as when I'd take a wrong turn behind the wheel, but also a life philosophy. That confidence had masked and, at times, made up for my many deficiencies of character, spotty education, and various moral failings. I hadn't realized how central this kind of sturdiness was to my identity until its absence cratered my equilibrium.

My neighborhood seemed to have shape-shifted, landmarks had rearranged themselves. I got lost on the way back from the grocery store where I'd shopped for twenty-five years. The store was less than a mile from our home.

I was so hesitant while driving that I became that unwitting menace on the road: the slowpoke driver. A few days after the Zoom with Dr. Sad Eyes, I exited a parking lot, drove forward, and, instead of pulling out into traffic, hesitated and was rear-ended. It was barely a tap, but I got out of the car and berated the driver. "How could you do this? I have cancer!"

The two middle-aged women in the other car were mercifully unflappable and attempted to reassure me. "It's not a big deal," the driver said. "It will be okay."

Our insurance companies handled it promptly, but I was not okay. My anxiety over driving became a nonissue because soon enough I didn't have a car.

It was a Sunday night just after midnight, three weeks after the fender bender, when I heard loud banging on the front door. Standing there was a bear of a man, sporting a Metallica T-shirt, unmasked at a time when most were still masking up, and clutching what looked to be a billy club.

"What's happening?" I wailed, sure it was a home invasion.

"I'm onto your game, lady," he said, stomping his shit-kicker boots up the driveway and toward my car.

"I don't understand," I cried out, trailing behind him.

He shouted something about my car being sold off at auction as he pulled out of the driveway. The tow truck's lights flashing and back-up beeping breaking the sound and light barrier that the pandemic had brought to nighttime. Ezra and Jake, Juel's son, appeared on the sidewalk in front of the house just in time to witness me sinking to my knees, begging for mercy. For all I know, Jake might have dematerialized, because I have zero recollection of where he went nor how Ezra got me back inside the house.

My memory kicks back in with this scene: I was prostrate on the kitchen floor, alternating between a high-pitched staccato shrieking and a low-droning whimper, as Ezra stroked my hair and attempted to console me by regaling me with tales of his reckless and ill-conceived exploits prior to getting sober during his first year of college.

"Scarred for life" is the phrase Ezra uses to describe the terror of witnessing my collapse. I'd been the unflappable-in-a-crisis parent since his birth. I'd taken a break from driving. Ezra hadn't learned to drive, not uncommon in his generation, and now I'd lost our only form of transportation during the pandemic? I'd failed myself even more profoundly. Growing up, time had slowed to a crawl each time my mother handed a salesclerk a credit card. I willed myself to invisibility while she dialed the bank to get approval and when one card was denied, tried again with another. My mother's features remained frozen until approval was granted or denied. I was never going to subject my child to that kind of instability.

I'd opted for a Covid-related lease extension and hadn't spotted that the automatic payments that had been in place for three years were no longer being deducted from my account. I'd also received no notification that I'd fallen two months behind, which is perfectly legal in many states in the country. Automobile financial services make more money by selling your car if you're in default, even by one day, than by alerting you that you're in arrears. Making the situation doubly worse was that, as compromised as I was, I was sure I'd kept track of my basic finances. Inability to manage my family's finances was another addition to the list of losses.

During my first in-person appointment with Dr. Sad Eyes a week later, I got a piece of potentially good news. I'd tested positive for the type of lung cancer for which there was a corresponding innovative treatment called a "biomarker targeted therapy." I'd never heard those three words strung together.

I'd prepared questions in advance. I'd pulled out my pen and notebook, ready to take notes. My sister was listening on the phone for good measure.

"Are there other options we should be considering? Should I seek a second opinion?" I asked.

"Any doctor would tell you the same thing." He sad-eyed me, shutting down my questions with his trademark sigh.

My sister, who has never met a problem she couldn't spreadsheet her way out of, asked whether I should schedule a mammogram. Like many people, I'd fallen behind on regular appointments during Covid.

"I don't think we need to worry about that now," he said.

We understood that to mean: *We already know the cancer that will kill her.*

I dead-man-walking-ed it out of there, determined to get a second opinion and never set foot in his office again.

I knew no one with lung cancer so I enlisted help. Tonya, a friend since we were roommates at Northwestern University's summer theater program for high-schoolers, managed to come up with a friend of a friend's ex-spouse. "What you need to know is that this doc I'm recommending has the bedside manner of an open grave," said Frank, my tangential connection to a second opinion oncologist. I gleaned that he had been in treatment for a few years, but I didn't ask Frank any questions out of fear that the answers would be upsetting. I had no other recommendations, the doctor was nearby, and an open grave seemed better than shovel-ready Sad Eyes.

"Now is the best time in history to be diagnosed with lung cancer," said my second-opinion oncologist, which seemed a tad optimistic and not at all open grave.

He drew a timeline of the history of advances in lung cancer treatment, where I came into the picture, and where the science was going. He wasn't Michelangelo, so it took all of three minutes.

Historically, surgery, chemo, and radiation were the only options for lung cancer patients. While early-stage lung cancer might be cured (typically lung cancer returns), late-stage patients like me had died a quick and painful death. The average five-year survival rate for lung cancer was 5 percent. At the time of my diagnosis, that was still officially the accepted statistic. Lung cancer, as of this writing, remains the number one cause of cancer-related death around the globe. But in the early aughts, scientists discovered that genetic mutations were "driving" the growth of certain kinds of lung cancer. I'd been fortunate enough to have tested positive for one of these mutations. In layman's terms, this is referred to as having a "genetic mutation" but the technical term is "oncogene-driven" cancer. Numerous targeted therapies, classified as tyrosine kinase inhibitors (TKIs), target and turn off the specific genes that have mutated—or, essentially, gone rogue.

There were two main classifications: small cell and non-small cell. I had tested positive for EGFR, epidermal growth factor receptor, mutated non-small cell lung cancer. The EGFR gene is the genetic code that makes the EGFR protein, a molecule that sits on the surface of cells and drives cell growth. Essentially these EGFR proteins, like disgruntled employees, were creating a toxic workplace environment and plotting a hostile takeover. In 2003, the first drug that inhibits EGFR's rogue behavior was developed. I'd be taking the targeted therapy osimertinib, sold under the brand name Tagrisso, which became standard protocol in the U.S. in 2018.

Only, this targeted therapy would be a temporary stopgap. Eighteen months was the average length of time the therapy remains effective before the cancer begins to metastasize again. My second-opinion oncologist described it in what I'd come to recognize as his inimitably vivid way: "Your cancer is a lawn. These medications keep the grass mowed, but they don't pull out the roots."

The one pill, once a day, would be our first line of treatment. Chemo, radiation, those would be the next. There were a limited number of choices because immunotherapy didn't work for my kind of cancer, though it did for other types. In the best-case scenario, while still incurable and deadly, my disease could be managed like a chronic illness. The average five-year survival rate for patients who responded to this class of miracle drugs was closer to 27 percent, but the oncologist advised not looking at statistics. The goal was to beat the clock, to stay alive long enough for when the cure arrives. Exciting trials were underway and people were living longer than what Dr. Google and Sad Eyes had indicated.

My sister teed up her mammogram question.

He listened, paused, and said, "I want to see you live long enough to *get* diagnosed with breast cancer. So, yeah, keep up the mammograms."

Okay, maybe that was the open grave, a plainspokenness bordering on tone deafness.

When I asked about the occasional glass of wine, he didn't hesitate.

"Sure, why not?"

I had a path forward. I had useful information. I had wine. I had one pill, once a day.

The best time in history turned out to be conditioned by a combination of luck and privilege. *If* you have access to testing for these mutations, *if* your local government has approved the treatment, *if* your insurer endorses your prescription, and *if* the meds work for you (not everyone responds to them), you've won a lottery ticket to longer survival.

After haggling with my insurance company and securing underwriting from the pharmaceutical's patient-assistance program, I was ready to try a miracle drug that can otherwise cost upward of seventeen thousand dollars a month on the open market and several thousand dollars a month for those with high-deductible insurance plans. This seemed to be what the pulmonologist had in mind when inquiring about my health insurance.

My big sister, Lisa, swooped in from the East Coast as I readied to start treatment. A poster child for birth order personality profiling, she runs a tight ship while I grow penicillin on cantaloupe that's been in my fridge for three years. I'd never felt more loved or terrified than when she told me she had purchased a one-way ticket to L.A.

For two months Lisa organized medical appointments, straightened out my finances, made spreadsheets of contact numbers for insurance companies, doctors, medications, and friends who'd offered to step into a caregiving role. She did all of this while getting up at 4 a.m. to put in a full day of remote work as the CEO of a multinational nonprofit and lavishing me with home-cooked meals.

T. S. Eliot wrote of measuring life in coffee spoons. I began measuring my life in three-month increments, which is how often this stealthy disease must be monitored through scans.

At the three-month mark, the tumors that at the time of diagnosis had been characterized as clementines, apricots, and walnuts had shrunk to the size of chickpeas, lentils, and kidney beans. Legumes were an improvement over fruits and nuts. I'd gotten an immediate response and the oncologist was pleased.

I was miserable.

Fatigue is a word that has always sounded poetic to my ear. I'd been told that fatigue was a possible side effect of the meds, but I'd associated the word with the French pronunciation, because *Je suis très fatiguée* was one of the few phrases that stuck with me from middle school French, and it conjured an image of loucheness. During a semester abroad in London, I'd swooned over the Pre-Raphaelites' renderings of doomed medieval damsels and sleepy-eyed star-crossed lovers. Even *Ophelia*, as envisioned by John Everett Millais, floating in a stream, festooned with flowers, and very fetching although dead, had a romanticized appeal to me. This was prior to my introduction to fatigue in the lexicon of cancer treatment.

If I got up in the morning to make coffee, the simple exertion of turning on the machine sent me crawling back to bed. If I sat down at my desk to write, by the time I powered up my computer, I needed a nap. The upside? I'd never been a great sleeper and I now had a superpower: I could fall asleep anytime, anywhere. *Sleep-deprived? Try cancer!* On certain days, I did have a good six or seven hours of wakefulness; unfortunately, none of those hours were consecutive. I wasn't sure this qualified as living. I was so fortunate, but so sleepy.

Little paper cuts on my fingertips and nail beds were an instant and daily affliction—vastly preferable to chemo side effects, but offering the lived experience of "death by a thousand cuts." This was a direct result of turning off the EGFR gene, which is associated with collagen production. No matter how much I drenched my skin in lotions and oils, extreme dryness caused fissures to open on the bottoms of my feet, making walking painful. I was waking up with blood-streaked arms and legs from scratching in my sleep. My scalp felt like it was on fire. "We've never heard of patients experiencing side effects so quickly after starting the medication," I was told by the office staff. They said that some patients experience raised welts and such severe full-body acne that the medication couldn't be tolerated. I sucked it up and stuck it out. I was so fortunate, but so itchy.

And, if you don't have curly hair prior to taking the targeted therapy, you can look forward to a new hair texture. Even the most Protestant Barbie-doll-blond hair acquires a semitic wiriness that defies every attempt at styling, but that was truly a minor event.

I could never have imagined being happy to hear my brain deemed unremarkable, but that's how a cancer-free brain is described. Now I had an unremarkable brain and hair. Woohoo!

I was having bouts of—there's no polite way of putting it—*Danger, Will Robinson, Danger*, no-lag-time diarrhea. Could you possibly stop by and open a bottle of Gatorade for me? I'll leave it outside of my front door, I texted my neighbors John and Randy, on a day I was so depleted from the loss of fluids that I didn't have the strength to twist off a plastic top. That night, I passed out on the bathroom floor in front of the commode. In order to avoid soiling myself, I'd stripped off my clothes and draped a towel over myself before losing consciousness. Ezra found me, restored me to a better state, and walked me to bed. That was the night he anointed me "Cancer Mom."

I didn't need to perform walking like a zombie anymore; I'd become one. I'm not suggesting this as a strategy, but if you're a parent looking to get your adult child out of your home, incontinence might do the trick. Not long after this episode, and with my blessing, Ezra, who'd found employment, moved into a nearby apartment with friends.

The bathroom incident, as it turned out, was not a one-off. I'd hit my limit.

After that discouraging first call about the skin rash, I hadn't told my oncologist about the severity of the side effects that I was enduring. Later, I learned that patients routinely underreport side effects out of fear they will seem ungrateful to be receiving such advanced medications and worry over having to move on to the more toxic remediations.

When I told the oncologist I was sleepwalking through my life, which now consisted of trips to and from the bathroom, he proposed halving the dosage. That it was even possible to lower the dosage wasn't something that had been mentioned.

Each day was a nail-biter. If the lower dose didn't work, I'd have burned off my first line of treatment, and just like those lifelines in the game show *Who Wants to Be a Millionaire?*, you get only so many. I'd catch myself holding my breath through the day, as if I might preserve my lungs by taxing them less.

T. S. Eliot was wrong about April being the cruelest month. That distinction belongs to December for anyone with a chronic illness in America. As 2020 turned to 2021, I discovered that the holiday season would now be a reminder how much my life and finances had been impacted. In the past, I'd scrambled to squeeze in outstanding appointments, hoping to stretch the time before the new year's resetting of deductibles. Now that I required close monitoring, gaming the system was a nonstarter. Pity the person who gets diagnosed in late December, faces a surge of bills, and then, come January 1, must start all over in meeting out-of-pocket costs. Just another of those things I'd never thought of in the *before days.*

At the first appointment after lowering the dosage, I was a nervous wreck.

"Huh. That might be something right there." He'd pulled up my scan and pointed at a small spot on his computer screen.

Several lifetimes seemed to pass before he continued.

"Did you ever live in New York?"

"Yes."

"Did you have cockroaches?"

"Yes." Where was he going with this?

"Well, cancer is like cockroaches. There's never just one," he said.

I held my breath, bracing myself for bad news and more troubling metaphors.

"Still stable. Break out the champagne."

In the airy, art-filled hospital, you can fool yourself into thinking you're at an Ian Schrager boutique hotel. Sure, there was someone hooked up to a portable oxygen tank, but they were seated on an Ole Wanscher couch. I floated from my oncologist's office, heading out under the *Distant Horizon*, a Baldessari outdoor installation. I was ready for some bubbly.

First, I was going to call Frank, share the good news, and thank him. But as I stepped into the parking structure, I deflated. Tonya called to let me know that Frank had died the night before. There was no guarantee that in three months, I wouldn't be joining Frank.

The End of My Life Is Killing Me

French fries! That certain slant of light! The scent of night jasmine! My appreciation of small pleasures was painfully acute. I was regularly overcome by almost inebriating episodes of gratitude overload. The pristine stabbing pain of an aspartame-induced diet soda headache! A Katherine Mansfield sentence could bring me to my knees. No, a Katherine Mansfield sentence should always bring us to our knees!

My complexion was rosy and my constitution, if powered by enough caffeine, energic. I'd been granted a temporary reprieve from death, but not from the overuse of exclamation points! With "eighteen months is the average time before the medication loses its effectiveness" replaying over and over in my head, as well as Frank's death ringing like a wake-up call, I hit the ground running, determined to carpe every diem.

Wasn't that the lesson imparted by those hovering at death's door? Suck the joy before shuffling off this mortal coil.

Side effects flared up, and then vanished altogether, allowing for fleeting moments of invincibility. One day, I stretched my afternoon walk into a satisfying but prostrating steep uphill climb. I was five blocks from home when I couldn't take another step. I crumpled like a wet potato chip onto a grassy meridian. Grassy meridians: What an extraordinary use of public space, I thought, lying there, inert and unable to rouse myself. Not a single passing car stopped to check on me. Half an hour later, I crab-walked my way home.

"Women in Los Angeles will do anything to stay fit—I saw one crawling on all fours down the sidewalk today!" I imagined someone regaling their dining guests that night.

I was undeterred! I was an urban landscape aficionado.

I dove into everything with a "just in case this is my last chance" energy. My rapprochement with bread was complete and joyous. Bread's BFF, butter, became my constant companion. I slathered it on everything, just in case it was my last chance to savor the wonder that is churned cow, sheep, and goat's milk. I got into plant-based butter, which isn't technically butter, it's an oil, but let's not split hairs.

I plotted my return to the activities that had animated my *before times.* For close to a decade, I'd helped high school seniors with their college essays at the local public school. The tutoring program was intended to level the playing field for students whose families couldn't afford private counselors.

Like with your own kids, you could devote hours, weeks, even months, working to meet midnight deadlines, only to have them become convinced they did it all themselves. But unlike your own progeny, they never called to remind you of that time you accidentally shut their finger in a window, invited their band for an extended stay at your home, or borrowed from your emergency earthquake funds and *neglected* to tell you. It was the ideal interaction with teenagers and a tonic for the highs and lows of a career in the arts.

By January 2021, schools were still closed, and even though we'd be working online, the school district now required fingerprinting. That's how I discovered that the grooves on my fingertips had faded—another, and uncommon, side effect of the medication. I'd never given my fingerprints much thought, but their absence seemed like a metaphor for the way cancer was threatening to erase me.

Was cancer robbing me of do-gooding?

I emailed friends to ask if they needed someone murdered. But, you know, only for a really good reason. Then brilliance struck: I could emancipate my favorite Yaacov Agam drawing from the prized art collection at my hospital. It hung in a dimly lit basement corridor, underappreciated. I could see it brightening the drab walls of the high school. I wouldn't be stealing, I would be *liberating* it for the students! I tested the security fastenings at my next scan. Twice. Just to be sure.

What was the worst that could happen? A life sentence?

In Thornton Wilder's classic American play *Our Town*, Emily, who has "had some trouble bringing a baby into the world," awakens to life's aching gorgeousness only after her untimely death. I portrayed Emily in high school, a performance for which thankfully no footage exists. "I didn't realize," Emily says in Act III, "so, all that was going on and we never noticed," and I was noticing it 24/7.

Each day brought a calamity of kindness.

I'd told only my inner circle, but after coming forward with my diagnosis in *The New York Times* and on *Good Morning America*, friends and distant connections sent cushy bathrobes and fuzzy slippers. A standout was a bathrobe, or more of a slanket—a blanket with sleeves. The faux leopard print, the train that trailed me by two feet, and the massive collar suggested the robe was modeled after coronation-style royal mantles. I paraded, holding court, when the newly informed came over for outdoor visits. Colleagues spanning many years reached out, as did childhood friends, and doctors who'd cared for Ezra as a baby.

There were some who reached out seeking confirmation that they hadn't done something that might lead them to suffer my fate. They quizzed me as to my lifestyle choices and dietary habits, and then murmured the appropriate condolences, apotropaic wardings off of my bad juju. But those were rare occurrences.

One morning, I awoke to find a vat of homemade matzoh ball soup on my doorstep. A childhood summer camp friend had dropped it off without stopping in just in case I wasn't up for company. It was still steaming.

Friends offered to launch a GoFundMe. I didn't anticipate needing one, but a longtime admirer of my work sent a check, as did a director I'd worked with once. The community choir I'd sung with for two decades collected money on my behalf and presented me with a check. We'd done this sort of thing in the past for others, but I never imagined being on the receiving end.

I twisted myself in knots over whether to return the money, but I knew that with the limitations of the pandemic, this was one of the few tangible gestures possible. It wasn't what you'd call life-changing; what it was was life-affirming. The generosity floored me. It reminded me of the delight my father took in palming fifty-dollar bills into his grandkids' hands like he was tipping a maître d'. He called it WHAM: Walking-Around Money (the H was for effect). I used the money to hire a get-your-affairs-in-order attorney and purchase a stupidly expensive sauna sleeping bag. Slipping inside was like a warm embrace, the closest thing to physical contact at that time.

A casting director I'd known since my twenties offered me a supporting role in a Michael Bay movie. The movie was one of the few in production at that time, and prior to vaccination, this was a risky proposition for someone with a serious respiratory illness, but I signed on just in case it was my last chance to practice my craft. Also, Bay's movies include the *Transformer* series and have some of the highest body counts in film history. Excluding *Armageddon*, where he wipes out much of the planet, the body count total is 9,087. Fans keep track. I said yes because wouldn't there be some morbid irony if I got to be number 9,088? I said yes because wouldn't there be some macabre irony if acting in a film titled *Ambulance* caused my death?

Millions of dollars are at stake every day on a big budget movie shoot, but this was nothing like any studio movie set I'd ever experienced. With Covid precautions in place, I'd be doing my own hair and makeup, and supplying my own wardrobe. There were security checkpoints to pass through, like a military operation. The cast members would be isolated and have rapid tests prior to being escorted to set. I'd be operating on someone else's schedule, unable to pivot if I had an episode of brain fog, fatigue, or that constant companion: gastric distress.

Getting to the set required passing through a maze of holding areas, cordoned off with plastic sheeting. We three cast members, Bay, and a skeleton crew assembled in an airless room. All venting had been shut down as a Covid precaution. To keep the crew tight, Bay would operate the camera himself. We counted down and unmasked. Now I felt naked and out of practice in comporting my facial expressions in the presence of others. Even Bay admitted to being nervous. This was the first indoor scene of the shoot. This was also the first time since the outbreak that I'd been unmasked with anyone other than Ezra and my sister and I'd chosen to do so, risking my life, on a film set.

I'd rehearsed my (few) lines in my scene as the couples therapist for a gay FBI agent and his partner, anxious about my memory, for hours. In a confusion that could happen only during Covid with a production team of this size, I landed in my nightmare scenario: The cast hadn't been sent the most recent revisions. I mainlined Diet Coke with its metallic caffeinated jolt to focus on the new lines. I barely scraped through. At least my impending death meant I'd never have to do that again, I told myself as I drove home.

I received proposals of marriage and other propositions. A *Times* reader who claimed to be a nurse with a generous health insurance plan offered to marry me. I saved her contact info. A man I hadn't seen in twenty years, who'd made a killing at a tech startup, flooded my phone with videos of his extensive art collection. I took this to be a wealthy man's version of dick pics. A platonic pal, who'd long held a torch, jumped on my declining health as an opportune moment for something adjacent to a mercy fuck, offering to be "my penis in the storm." A college boyfriend going through a messy divorce wrote to send condolences on my impending death and to reconfirm that "we'd once been in love, hadn't we?" I reminded him he'd cheated on me with my best friend.

So, should I try my hand at love, or lust, just in case it was my last chance? But who would date someone facing a "poor outcome"?

Someone with commitment issues. Or maybe, I reasoned, someone who also had cancer. I googled "cancer dating," which yielded two promising leads. The first was designed for people so compromised they were seeking relationships without physical intimacy. I wish I could report that it was called "No Skin in the Game," but it was actually something like "Hand-Holding Only" and administrated by someone describing themselves as "sex-c." I applaud this sensitive and inclusive-minded undertaking, but I clicked over to the second site, which matched cancer folk by location.

There were 890 cancers in my zip code. That sounded like a cluster warranting further investigation by the NIH and almost enough cancers to polish off that vat of matzoh ball soup. I scrolled for twenty minutes before I realized: this site was for *Cancers*, the astrological sign. Wait, statistically speaking, shouldn't some of these Cancers have cancer?

Then, out of the blue, I reconnected with an old crush IRL.

I'd known him in passing when my son was in grade school; he was a father of twins who were a year younger than Ezra. I'd noted his rakish Daniel Craig–ish good looks and a "take your pants off" British-Kiwi accent. The imperious British lilt, tempered by the salt-of-the-earth sturdy twang of those who make their home on the rugged, primordial terrain of Aotearoa. He and his wife had recently separated. He'd moved nearby, and after a month of hiking the local trails and playing badminton in my backyard, Jeremy and I went out for dinner. I'd been sure that he was looking for a hiking buddy, but over dessert, he confessed in a low wanton growl to having glimpsed the shape of my ass when I'd bent down to retrieve a shuttlecock during one of our matches.

My backside was never my strong suit, or rather body part. One of the cheeks of my posterior rests a tad to noticeably lower than the other side. Let's not use the word *hangs* or *droops*, because that would be too dramatic, but a former boyfriend once noted with astonishment that my otherwise fit frame was blessed with an ass unblemished by even the minutest amount of muscle tone. During our time together, he pledged to quit drinking and partaking in drugs, activities he pursued with enthusiasm and vigor, if I agreed to work out. Years later, he died of an overdose, and although I know it wasn't my fault, occasionally I'll wonder: Would it have hurt to have done a few Jane Fonda butt lifts?

My behind was an oft-discussed topic throughout my marriage. As wedded bliss sank into wedded blah, the threshold for things better left unsaid sank lower, as did my behind, apparently. When my ex dubbed it the "sad left cheek," I'd laughed. It stung, but contempt had become our love language.

I took to carefully concealing the so-called SLC when alighting tout nude from the marital bed. Swathing it, swaddling it, and in general sashaying in a locomotion designed to prevent the offending lower backage from bringing anyone else down by virtue of its existence became second nature. At this late stage of life, was redemption within reach?

I threw myself at Jeremy with *just in case this was my last chance* enthusiasm. After our first assignation, I was about to cover up the SLC, as is my habit, when Jeremy sighed, "Can I see your glorious ass one more time?"

I pivoted, nude, and treated him to an unobstructed view of the sad left cheek in all its floppy majesty, and excused myself to use the bathroom. Whether I had another day or another decade was uncertain. But I knew one thing: I was never walking backward to the bathroom again.

"You have honeymoon cystitis," my gynecologist said at my next visit. This term for a UTI, still regularly invoked by medical professionals, is informed by Victorian notions of chastity, assuming that the first time a woman has sexual intercourse is on her honeymoon. "The trauma of vaginal penetration," as my gynecologist relishes labeling it, causes little tears in the vaginal membrane, allowing for bacteria to enter the system.

If you've never had a UTI, consider yourself an anomaly and also extremely fortunate. Along with the sensation that your bladder is trying to burst through your abdomen, *Alien* style, you not only feel like you have to pee all the time; you do have to pee all the time. And it's painful.

"Annabelle, you need to stop having so much sex," my gynecologist admonished me. Two months into the "just in case" affair, I'd shown up again, doubled over in discomfort.

"Cancer is my bad boyfriend, and I'm cheating on him with joy."

Later that night, Jeremy whispered, "Maybe, I'll be your last." Only later did I realize he'd sweetly floated the possibility of a long-lasting love, because I'd interpreted it as "given your projected lifespan."

Which was good, because I was only interested in a last-chance liaison. Starting a new relationship later in life, even if you're not facing a known health threat, raises the question: What is it that you want if you're not going to have a family together or aren't building a life together?

You could look at the data that support the premise that women invest in their female friendships more than men, who tend to lean on their spouses, or you could just look to the number of "let's all live together one day in a bestie row of tiny houses" memes on the internet to understand why women my age often eschew romantic relationships. It's not dudes who are pictured in quaint locations wearing Lululemon athleisure. My lifelong friendships were time-tested.

And how much did Jeremy and I know about each other? Not a lot, practically speaking, and that was the best part. I'd been upfront about my diagnosis and prognosis, but I didn't need to know about the ins and outs of his recent separation, and he didn't need to know about all of the side effects and close monitoring.

I wanted to drift through the fog of romance for as long as possible. Had I accidentally found a special someone with commitment issues?

Friends recommended probiotics, prebiotics, and even postbiotics, and I stockpiled cranberry juice, but all to no avail, before adjusting to the reality that UTIs were inescapable and I'd be taking antibiotics almost continually, despite the risk of eventually becoming antibiotic resistant. This is one of those unexpected gifts. With a very likely shortened lifespan, I decided: fuck it.

In the meantime, people with serious health issues became eligible for vaccines. Between Covid and the uncertainty of the medication, this might be my last ambulatory opportunity to see my cherished friends.

I drove to Cal State Los Angeles, the designated large-scale vaccination site. The parking lot was manned by soldiers administering the vaccines. I waited for an hour in a line of cars and then I rolled down my window and took in the uniformed person with excellent posture, zero facial hair, and a trace of baby fat.

"Where are you from? How old are you? Your parents must be proud of you."

"Arizona. (Or, maybe, New Mexico?) Nineteen. Yes, ma'am."

I told the soldier I had cancer (I was telling everyone within earshot at that time), that I had a child around his age, that he was saving my life, that I was so grateful. He jabbed my left arm and handed me my stamped vaccination passport. I wept all the way home.

On the fourteenth day after receiving the vaccination, the recommended time for immunity to kick in, I double-masked it to the airport. I arrived five hours prior to the flight. I'd misread my reservation or made the wrong reservation. I'm still not sure. I attempted to metabolize the mistake. I took a nap, sitting upright at a restaurant table, and then made my way over to my gate with plenty of time to spare. The gate was packed. I hadn't been in a crowd in over a year. Wary about exposure and disoriented by the loudness of the announcements, I lagged behind in the line and suddenly, or so it seemed, the flight was closed.

My pulse racing, my brain short-circuited. I called my sister, worried that I might spiral into a full-blown panic attack and require medical attention.

"Lisa, can you stay on the phone with me until I board the next flight?"

My sister was in the middle of her workday. She kept her phone on speaker for three hours, until my flight took off. I listened to her tapping away on her computer, taking and making calls on another phone, tethered to her, electronically, not unlike when we were children and our mother would clip our mittens together—I'd been a runner.

The trees on the Upper West Side were in full bloom. Every morning for a week, I trekked to "my" table at Le Monde. I'd scheduled one meetup for each day: Heather, Neena, Tonya, Annie, Jessica. Heather and I had been attached at the hip since grade school. Neena and Tonya had entered my life as teenagers and never left. Annie and I had met in college; we'd raised our children together before she moved back to New York, and we observed an annual swim every summer in the Atlantic near her home in Martha's Vineyard. Jessica and I hadn't met until our twenties, but seemed to have always been soul sisters.

All around us, other diners were observing their own first-time-since-Covid reconvening. The hugging and the tears and the rising swiftly and yet somehow in slow-motion to greet each other. The joy was infectious and spilled over from table to table. Cherry blossoms swirled like confetti enveloping us in clouds of Capezio pink. Our reunions careened between celebratory and funereal as we brunched our way down memory lane. These meals lasted hours, our farewells wrenching, as this was possibly what writer and cancer survivor Kate Bowler calls "the great goodbye."

Each day, blurry-eyed, I'd walk back to Jessica's place, where I was staying, flattened for the remainder of the day.

In *Our Town*, Emily revisits formative moments at her childhood home in Grover's Corners before taking her place in the cemetery among the dead. New York City was my first love and I would do that too.

"Goodbye, world," Emily says, the first of her farewells.

"Goodbye, Le Monde," I said, and set off toward downtown.

"Goodbye, Grover's Corners . . . and Mama and Papa . . . Goodbye to clocks ticking . . . And food and coffee and new-ironed dresses and hot baths . . ."

Goodbye, rats of 109th Street, rattiest street of the Upper West Side. Remember the night I hopscotched my way from Columbus to Broadway and managed to avoid you all, except for that one?

Goodbye, Apthorp Building, storied home of Nora Ephron. I'd pined to live within your Italian Renaissance Revival walls, but never managed, not even once, to get invited inside your stately—and since those new owners, slightly garish—gates.

Goodbye, 255 West Seventeenth Street. Oh, to have those hours spent waiting behind that police barricade to hunt down bargains at the Barneys warehouse sales. I still have the detachable strap from a boho bag I scored once, cause a good strap is hard to find.

Goodbye, 170 West Twelfth Street, former site of St. Vincent's Hospital, where my friends succumbed to AIDS in the '80s, leaving me so bereft I felt compelled to move west.

Goodbye, 325 Rear West Fourth Street, my dilapidated carriage house home of five years, a studio without a closet or kitchen sink but with a slanted floor and an alcoholic neighbor fond of wrapping her panties around my front doorknob. Every brownstone on the block has been handsomely refurbished, but not you. Your vestibule is strewn with detritus, the entryway window smashed, you're exactly as shitty as the day I departed in 1989.

Too tired to continue walking, I descended into the Christopher Street subway station. As I stepped onto the platform, something splashed onto my calf. It wasn't raining outside. Oh, New York, you offered me your secret sauce. An unexpected wet. What are you: Urine, holy water, the collected sweat of all of those who dream of making it here?

"Oh, earth, you're too wonderful for anybody to realize you," thought this once-and-forever Emily.

Emily sits down in her chair in the cemetery "waitin'," the stage manager tells us. "Waitin' for the eternal part . . . to come out clear," he says.

Back at Jessica's, I lay on the sofa and looked out at the Hudson River. I'd said my goodbyes. I'd carped every diem. I was waitin' too. Not for the eternal part, but for an answer as to how I was going to survive my impending death.

In just under a year, I'd gone from shipwrecked to ecstatic and everything in between. I'd exhausted my range of emotions and graduated to an even more stultifying state: numbness.

I missed my flight home. I'd misread my ticket, again, this time arriving at the airport too late. Back home in Los Angeles,

I unraveled, like the elastic band of my mother's swirling blue 1970s Pucci half-slip. It held on for forty years. Then, one day, it just gave out.

It was all I could do to form a single cogent thought: the end of my life is killing me.

You Had Me at We Should

"I can't go on. I'll go on." *Texts for Nothing*, one of Samuel Beckett's many meditations on the human condition, begins with those two sentences. In this tragicomedy, a typical Beckettian everyman is trapped in a limbo. Has he been there for an hour or a lifetime, who can say?

When an acting teacher of mine at NYU performed this as a monologue in 1981, I laughed out loud. I assumed Beckett's work was hyperbole, a theatrical spectacle. I was eighteen and still believed that good skin and boundless ambition would provide easy passage through life.

I couldn't have imagined that one day a gaping chasm might open up between those sentences that perfectly described my predicament. When Beckett becomes relatable, you're in dire straits.

The rest of *Texts for Nothing* never made a lick of sense to me, but a decision seemed to have been made, some thought process or approach that transformed *I can't* into *I will.* What would that shift look like? What would it cost me? I couldn't fathom.

This is why Beckett is so disorienting. His characters are stuck in repetitive loops, Godot never shows. And still, they go on, even if that means more waiting.

Beckett lived until eighty-three. If his life were the model, I'd be passing my afternoons rakishly attired in turtlenecks, throwing back black coffees, smoking cigarettes, and spooling out Nobel Prize–winning works at Café de Flore in Paris. I hadn't been to Paris in two decades and wasn't blessed with Beckett's brilliance.

So, how to go on?

The newly diagnosed often get caught up in the why of it all. Why me? I wasn't under any illusion that the universe works in anyone's favor, so mine was more of a *how* problem. I'd muscled through challenges by sheer force of will, but both my go-getter instincts and my resolution to live each day like it was my last had crashed and burned.

"We tell ourselves stories in order to live," Joan Didion wrote; we impose narrative lines "to freeze the shifting phantasmagoria of actual experience."

We like our stories tidy. We take comfort in beginnings, middles, and endings. Preferably upbeat ones. We want to know that if we follow this course of action, and then that one, and if necessary, another one after that, just to be sure we've covered all our bases, then we'll have a good outcome. Light at the end of the tunnel. But the story I found myself in promised all tunnel. No light. Could I find a way to make the best of it, to make it a clean, well-lighted tunnel?

Meanwhile, I was bogged down with another quagmire. My husband and I were on our third attempt at mediation. Why had our marriage ended after two decades? The math would not hold. Our grievance list outnumbered our gratitude list, and we couldn't reverse the equation. Math wasn't either of our strong suits. We'd been living separate lives since Ezra went to college, and our first two attempts to finalize things had gone off the rails for every reason imaginable. Mainly, worried over the financial fallout of divorce, I preferred to stay married, but my husband had different plans. He'd already entered another relationship, which I didn't know at the time.

We'd launched the third round when Covid hit. Our mediation moved to Zoom. Then came the diagnosis.

"How are you doing?" the mediator would ask at the top of our scheduled sessions.

"How do you think I'm doing? I have stage four cancer!" I didn't have it in me to obey the niceties of social interactions. After sobbing my way through a couple of sessions, I suggested we hit pause. My husband wanted to press on. We'd negotiated almost all of the points of contention, but I couldn't sign anything in this state. That constant oscillation, *zozobra,* had paralyzed my decision-making capabilities. I had cancer and was getting divorced?

I can't go on; I can't go on.

Each mediation was a reminder of the loss of the marriage, which was a reminder of the loss of my health. I was in a Beckettian loss loop. I wanted to focus on what I still had: a strong support network, including two friends from my theater tribe who stepped back into my life after a long absence.

Jill, Sarah, and I met in 1990. We were all recent transplants from Manhattan, pursuing careers in the entertainment business in Los Angeles. Sarah, ten years younger than Jill and me, was an actress and writer and recent college grad. Jill had been a dancer with a prestigious modern dance company. We formed a collective that met every Tuesday night for two years in a run-down rehearsal space in Hollywood. In a display of our collective imagination, we dubbed it the Tuesday Group. There were eight of us in this loose affiliation. Each brought skills we'd acquired to the group: improv exercises, stage combat, plays to read. We studied dance and tai chi. All of us were the first in our friend groups to move across the country, and like expats who didn't speak the native language, we clung to each other like life rafts.

As we found employment and established other connections, we disbanded, but we kept in intermittent touch. Jill and I had children at the same time. As babies, they were inseparable until they went to different schools. Jill became the drama and dance teacher at our local high school and recruited me into the college essay mentorship program. When Sarah gave birth to twins ten years later, she was sidelined by a bacterial infection. Jill and I stopped in for a visit. While Sarah napped, Jill and I folded laundry.

"We won't be seeing her for a while," Jill said, after we'd said our goodbyes.

It took fifteen years and my cancer diagnosis to get the three of us together again.

After I returned from New York in the summer of 2021, we reconnected and picked up right where we'd left off. We began gathering in my backyard on Sundays, every two to three weeks, for tea and sympathy, and a little badminton thrown in to boot. Jill and Sarah brought their dogs, Cotton and Chunk, to play together as the local parks were closed at that time. They were the first to be treated to my fashion shows, modeling the many robes I'd received. Sunday Friends is how we referred to our little klatch. We weren't in contact between Sundays, we weren't that kind of confidants. Like church ladies at a reception after services. Only without the church.

Politics makes strange bedfellows and so does impending mortality. Of all the chosen families—cosplayers, video gamers, knitting circles, and tech bros—I'd argue that theater folk form the most durable bonds. Particularly if you've survived your salad days. Say you're doing a play in an unheated basement during winter; you're being paid so little that it's costing you money, the reviews are lousy, there are more people in the cast than there are in the audience, and still the show must go on. You're bonded for life.

Before my diagnosis, actors I hadn't spoken to in years would phone and two weeks later their kid would be living in my guest bedroom. Jill, Sarah, and I were theater folk, so the suddenness of Sunday Friends didn't make sense, but it also didn't not make sense; they were my people.

We were ahead of the trend of setting regularly scheduled friendship dates. In recent years, this approach to building closeness has been highlighted in a slew of articles. Researchers compare its effectiveness to the way that an exercise routine takes hold only through consistent calendaring. In a *New York Times* essay titled "The Secret to Deeper Friendships Is in Your Calendar," Stefano Montali traces this to a German tradition of Stammtisch, or a "regulars' table," where bars reserve a table for familiar faces to gather and socialize.

One Sunday, I was awaiting the creak of the backyard gate announcing their arrivals when that now-familiar wave of fatigue hit. I lay face down on the grass and listened to the singing of the spotted towhees that make their home in my sprawling maple. I've read this kind of thing has become popular; practitioners call it "grounding" or "earthing," but I was simply stretching out on a patch of grass, like humans have done for centuries prior to the invention of that world-changing technology: the couch.

Jill showed up first and, without a word, dropped the bag of lemons she'd brought over and joined me on the ground. Then Sarah showed up and followed suit. Over tea, we laughed about how neither had asked, "What are we doing?" or "How long are we going to be here?" "What's next? Ritualistic purification rites? Animal sacrifice?" They'd simply joined in.

As we said our goodbyes, I said, "You know what we should do—"

"Yes!" Sarah said before I'd even finished the sentence.

"You don't even know what I was going to say."

"Annabelle, you had me at *we should*."

That's how I'll go on, I thought.

In comedy improv, there's a golden rule: say "yes, and." If you can't agree on what scene you're in, the action can't move forward. You're about to announce that you're a dentist preparing to launch into ye-ole-maniacal-madman-with-a-drill routine, but your scene partner has just brandished a gladius and scutum. If you don't join this gladiator in the Colosseum, all momentum is going to grind to a halt. In life, it's much harder. I've rarely said yes to anything without intense deliberation.

Sarah's willingness had a certain ease. Would ease ever be possible again? Was Jill's giving in to gravity a model for giving in to the gravity of my situation? It jogged a memory of something Mel Gottlieb, a former therapist, often repeated. Mel was an adherent of the early-twentieth-century Austrian psychoanalyst Otto Rank, a contemporary of Freud. Rank described something he called "the volitional affirmation of the obligatory." In essence, fighting the reality of your circumstance creates tension. Instead of going kicking and screaming, why not go with the flow? The "volitional" part is key; it's the acknowledgment that acceptance is a choice. The affirmation is an act of will. Maybe "You had me at we should" was the practical backyard bridge building between *I can't go on* and *I'll go on*.

The first opportunity to put this to the test came almost immediately, in the form of another message asking to continue the mediation. I said yes, even though I wanted to say no. No one got everything they wanted and compromises were made, like in every divorce settlement in the history of the world, and settling our affairs provided a punctuation mark that interrupted the existential slide into divorce-related despair.

I don't recommend a Zoom divorce. An online ending grants you the opportunity to observe your partnership's devolution in two-dimensional starkness: bodies that once shared space and time, partitioned into distinctly demarcated territories—boxes—not unlike how your respective belongings have been divided. You and the person you could recognize by scent alone are now suspended in an antiseptic ether, just to reinforce the reality that what you once considered foundational has etherealized. One, or both of you, will freeze, reliably, into an impenetrable version of yourself, trapped in time, preserved in cyber-amber. Take a screenshot. It will serve as a twenty-first-century fossilized record of your marriage's end that you can later revisit. That is, if you can remember where you saved the recording, which you won't. And when your internet goes down mid-session, which it will, "connection lost" will appear on your screen, as if you weren't already aware of that.

The Sunday Friends Stammtisch became another kind of scaffolding. The regularity cementing our bond. We have a text chain to check in on each other. We send poems and favorite passages from books we're reading. If someone is going through a really rough patch, we'll send that universal cure-all: GIFs of interspecies love—a racoon riding an alligator, a gorilla cradling a kitten, a cat cuddling with a mouse, a capybara riding an alligator. We're those *ride or die* friends, even though that's a terrible phrase you don't want to contemplate too deeply.

Because the moral arc of the universe bends toward irony, the inspiration for "You had me at we should" didn't pan out as expected. I'd meant to suggest that day in my backyard that Sarah, Jill, and I take a friend up on a generous offer to spend a restive weekend at his mountain retreat on the edge of the San Bernardino National Forest. It took some wrangling, but we pulled it off. Sort of. Jill and I spent two lazy days sleeping late, reading, and hiking. But Sarah, with her younger kids still living at home, had last-minute parental responsibilities that prevented her from joining us.

"Whatever you do with this time in your life, be sure to make a mess of it," Claudette, a longtime role model who is a bit my senior, advised me when I told her about my newfound approach.

That Sarah hadn't made it to the retreat seemed a perfect expression of this messy, imperfect way forward.

I Feel You, Persephone

In Greek mythology, the maiden Persephone was plucking the day away, picking violets and bright white lilies in a sylvan meadow, when suddenly the ground opened up and she was spirited away to the subterranean lair of Hades, king of the underworld. Hades had become obsessed with making Persephone his wife. He was her uncle, so that's creepy, but he was undeterred by that minor inconvenience, and promptly ensconced her as his queen.

I was sixty, decidedly not maiden material, when the foundation of my life crumbed. But I feel you, Persephone.

Since their invention, the gods and goddesses have provided archetypes for ethical behavior and aspirational benchmarks. We mortals sweat over Sisyphean tasks, indulge in bacchanalian revelry; even the crowning of athletes and graduates with laurel wreaths owes a nod to Mount Olympus. We ascribe meaning to our vicissitudes by mapping parallels to epic journeys, like the one undertaken by Odysseus on his decade-long odyssey to return home to Ithaca after the Trojan Wars. The hero's journey was co-opted by the self-help movement and is now ubiquitous, conferring significance on every manner of passage.

The internet is lousy with journeys.

"My fertility journey," "my journey to financial freedom," "my weight-loss journey," "my divorce journey." There's an entire category of Instagram accounts devoted to "my nail growth journey."

Whenever someone uses the word *journey*, I want to punch them. And yet, it's practically mandated that the mental gymnastics, financial jujitsu, and physical hoops you must jump through in order to stay alive are collectively referred to as your *cancer journey*. Even though I resisted that labeling, I felt like I was straddling two worlds, with one foot in the grave and another on terra firma, so it seemed natural to consider Persephone's plight.

Fortunately for Persephone, her mother Demeter, Goddess of the Harvest, was a *balabusta*, the Yiddish term for ballbuster. Let's just call her an indomitable matriarch. Bereft at the prospect of her daughter's eternal confinement to the underworld, she brokered a deal between Zeus, her husband and Persephone's father, and Hades. Persephone was granted a reprieve: She would split her time between the underworld and the land of the living. Her triumphant return was seen as a harbinger of spring; her annual descent heralded the onset of winter.

Carl Jung's interpretation of the myth of Persephone was that it represented the transitory nature of joy and suffering. Jung argued that continually cycling through periods of darkness and light was endemic to the human condition. That made sense, I was cycling between intense emotional states, but along with the metaphorical, I took something more practical from Persephone's predicament: It helps to have a staunch advocate in your corner. But who would be my Demeter?

After the initial showering of love and juicers, the dynamics in my support network got more complicated. The temporary reprieve offered by precision medications was still such an astonishing and new improvement in quality of life for someone with metastasized cancer that it was hard, even for me, to wrap my head around how I could have an incurable disease with a poor prognosis but appear to be the picture of health.

That I had a full head of hair and hadn't lost weight was a continuing source of confusion. The assumption that a chronic and in all probability deadly disease presents visually is a deeply ingrained cognitive dissonance in our culture and likely evolutionarily advantageous. My robustness elicited stupefying responses from even my most well-intentioned friends.

"Are you sure you have cancer? You don't have the cancer look," a friend insisted, mistaking the effect of some treatments for the disease itself.

"I'm sorry I don't look sick enough for you" turns out to be a reliable conversation stopper and an effective way to alienate your loved ones.

In the past, I'd sign up for meal trains and accompanied friends and neighbors to medical appointments. People offered to do that for me. While it might have been helpful for someone to run errands, I knew I could expect to have this Sword of Damocles (more imagery dating back to the Hellenistic Era) hanging over my head for many years to come, if I was lucky enough to be granted that much time. I didn't want to tire folks out so I didn't accept any of those kinds of kindnesses.

My immediate needs were less quantifiable. Plan A was the one-pill-a-day regimen, after which there were anticipated plans B, C, and D, until presumably planning a memorial service, and I didn't need assistance getting the one pill a day into my mouth.

Friends tried to bolster my resolve, and I managed to pick fights with almost all of them. When we talked, if someone sounded upbeat, I'd mention the statistical likelihood of impending death. If someone sounded negative, I'd feel compelled to be positive. "None of us knows what's ahead; I could get hit by a bus tomorrow" was the most maddening of well-meaning sentiments, because the bus had already run me over and was dragging me behind it. "You do know, along with having cancer, I could also get hit by a bus, so it's like I could double die" was not a response anyone wanted to hear.

When someone close to you is reminded of their mortality, it brings home your own impermanence.

My friend Annie's reaction was "You can't die. You promised me you'd put a pillow over my face if I ever get dementia!"

"I could put that pillow over you right now, if you'd like," I replied.

In addition to disease management and forensic medical billing accountant, I assumed another unpaid position: grief counselor for those mourning my impending demise. "I got this," I repeated, adopting a performative indefatigability.

I even picked a fight with my sister. Two months into her 24/7 Mary Poppinsing, she cheerfully announced, "Tonight, we're having homemade turkey zucchini loaf!"

"Blech, isn't it bad enough that I have cancer? Am I down to loaves too?"

Maggie, a writer friend with a Zen practice, recommended an app inspired by the Bhutanese teaching: to be a happy person, think about death five times a day.

The app sounded hilarious and like the right kind of entry-level *seeing things as they truly are* first-three-pages-of-Buddhist philosophy I was craving.

"It's called WeCroak."

"Sign me up," I replied.

WeCroak's invitation to contemplate my mortality arrived, as promised, "at random times, just like the real thing." While brushing my teeth: *Don't forget that you're toast!*

On my birthday, surrounded by loved ones singing happy birthday: *You're a goner!* "Are you sure?" my friend Heather asked, worried over my insistence on having NOT DEAD, JUST RESTING piped onto the triple-berry, freshly hand-whipped yellow buttercream birthday cake that she'd splurged on.

The alerts had revived the sharp, sour seduction of black comedy that the diagnosis had dulled. If I was going to double die, I might as well double down on the death humor.

When asked how I was doing, my go-to answer was "Doing great, but still scheduled to die!" The glee with which I delivered these responses didn't produce the guffaws I'd anticipated.

"You find it funny," my sister said, "but for people who love you, it can be hard."

I felt the stirring of something that scared me more than any amount of existential dread. Existential relief. At least if I die soon, I won't outlive my kid. Or my money. The only thing worse than outliving your child would be becoming burdensome to him. If there was an upside, this was it.

My sister and I had seen our parents through the worry of dwindling resources in their last years. My father was always certain that the big win was just around the corner. He and my mother had weathered boom times and busts. Still, we were stunned by the precariousness of their situation. By the end, they were subsidizing their Social Security benefits with "raincoat money." We'd assumed that this meant a rainy-day savings account. But no, that was how they referred to the cash from dad's poker winnings that they stashed in the pocket of an old Burberry raincoat.

Entertaining the saving graces of death felt shameful. I confided this to no one, which was further isolating. Particularly lonely were scan days. The miraculousness of my miracle drug was tempered by the thudding reality that each day on the medication subtracted a day from its effectiveness. Because I could be asymptomatic when progression occurred, I likened the scans to pilgrimages to the Oracle of Delphi.

On the days leading up to these visits, I was racked by "scanxiety." In preparation, friends forwarded oppressively upbeat TikToks featuring cancer survivors climbing Mount Everest or burst into tears at the sound of my voice. I declared a moratorium on receiving TED Talks given by people with cancer who had completed their first marathon. I needed someone to talk to without triggering emotional distress: mine and theirs.

I can't recall how I first heard about Imerman Angels, a cancer support community that matches mentors and mentees with the same conditions. I wasn't support group averse, but angels? As a nonbeliever, that's the last thing I was looking for. Their logo was a pair of wings. That seemed ill-advised. "Getting your wings" is a common euphemism for a poor outcome.

Still, I filled out the form. In the winter of 2020, an email introducing me to my angel, Hardye Moel (pronounced "hardy mole") landed in my inbox. Angels, wings, and now I was being paired with a small furry mammal? Was this a jokey nom de cancer about being a tough little critter?

Hardye followed up with an email encouraging me to call, text, or email.

An internet search yielded a photograph of a dapper gentleman fox-trotting with a petite blond woman. He had a distinctly mole-like bushy mustache. I'd requested to be matched with a female. Wasn't it enough that I'd asked for help from a stranger? I ignored the invitation to connect. But after that roller-coaster ride of a day when I learned my treatment was stable and that Frank had died, I was desperate for camaraderie.

I returned to the Imerman Angels website to read more about what I might be getting into. "Offering support at any stage of your journey," it said.

Angels and wings and journeys, oh my.

It took another eight months before I responded to Hardye's email. What would speaking with a stranger open me up to? What if they offered hopes and prayers?

"I've been having a hard time dealing with a death in our community," I wrote in an email requesting to set up a call in the fall of 2021.

Hardye, it turned out, was the female fox-trotter. During our first call, I learned that she was Chicago-based, had children, grandchildren, a wide circle of devoted friends, and an adoring spouse. Like me, she was both Jewish and a nonbeliever. And she was a practicing psychotherapist. Maybe there was a God after all! Mr. Moel was her third and favorite husband and adopting his surname was such a ridiculous proposition that she couldn't resist. At seventy-three, she'd been living with the disease for four years. She was tiny—under five feet tall—but a dynamo.

On the phone, I railed against the battling cancer metaphors and the exhortations to summon Herculean strength. I'd be letting everyone down, including myself, if I didn't measure up to those superhuman standards.

"I'm already in a competitive business," I said. "My goal is to be an underachiever at cancer. Cancer warrior? Can't I be a cancer slacker?"

Hardye laughed.

"I've taken a pledge," I continued. "No runs, no ribbons, no religion."

As far as existential relief was concerned, she related to not wanting to burden her family. We vowed to never send "hopes and prayers" to each other. Miraculously, Imerman Angels had manifested my perfect match.

She was the perfect scanxiety cell phone companion. She was on a similar, ugh . . . journey, and knew how enervating supporting your support team could be. The drive to the hospital took an hour. Hardye, my fellow traveler, journeyed with me, remaining on speakerphone the entire time. Neither lotus eater nor nihilist, her reassuring reminders that she'd had four stable years might be offset with "Oops, phone died. At least it wasn't one of us!"

With Hardye on speed dial, interactions with friends and family became less pressurized. It seemed only natural that she was the person to turn to for advice after I began seeing Jeremy. As hard as it was to contemplate sharing my life with someone new, even more daunting was the prospect of sharing my death.

Hardey granted me permission to take actions in the short term—a "just for now" approach, and my septuagenarian angel assured me that I could be "in it just for the sex."

I'd draw a hard line between Eros and Thanatos.

"How's the BF?" became her standard greeting.

By the winter of 2022, Hardye had a bad bout of Covid, and other more obtuse ailments: indigestion, dramatic weight loss, erratic heart rate. Long-term use of the medication takes a toll, making it difficult to distinguish between the cancer metastasizing and your body just wearing down. We had a lag in communication, and when she missed a scan-day call, I fretted over her health. Her medication—the same single pill that I took—stopped working. Her disease progressed, and she began chemotherapy. She worried about how I'd take the news. We both knew that her decline portended my own. When Hardye finally did reach out, she texted a picture of herself smiling during a chemo infusion, giving the camera a thumbs-up. The only good thing about today was my hair. Her blond bob as indefatigable as her spirit.

I assumed she was rallying until she sent an email with the subject line: "Cluster Fuck."

"Your angel fell apart," she wrote. Another bout of Covid, chronic fatigue, and the chemo had ravaged her body; she was exhausted and her weight slipped under ninety pounds. She decided: quality over quantity—no more treatment, only palliative care. "Don't feel like you need to keep talking to me," she wrote.

By now, we'd traded book recommendations, talked politics, shared stories about our children, and were signing off every exchange with heart emojis and love yous. Applying her "just for now" attitude to my daily life had made the debilitating worry over the future more bearable; I felt strong enough to pay it forward.

"It's hard for me to talk about this," she wrote. "After six great years, this feels like shit." She urged me to pursue joy. She encouraged a return to writing, travel, and cranberry juice. She connected me with support groups. Like Demeter wresting Persephone from the shadowy realm, Hardye restored me to the world of the living.

With my next scan day approaching, I sent a picture of me and Jeremy and asked if she was well enough for a phone call.

"How's the BF?" she asked as soon as she picked up. She was spending time with loved ones. Although she was in a good deal of pain, her voice sounded stronger; she was eager for laughs.

"I crossed the line with the BF," I said.

I explained how I'd gone for my regular scan, without mentioning it to Jeremy, as per usual, but I'd registered a dangerously low blood oxygen level while my vitals were being taken. They rushed me into additional scans and supplemental oxygen. It was so anxiety making, I'd taken a Klonopin and couldn't drive home. I called Jeremy. Between the nervousness, low oxygen level, drugs, and being wheeled into an imaging center on a gurney as a nurse hooked me up to an IV, I was giggling the entire time. He was on speakerphone and could hear me as I explained to the nurses that we'd just started sleeping together and that he didn't know I was at a hospital. Jeremy was a great sport about the whole thing. He Ubered an hour and a half northeast of Los Angeles to the facility to pick me up, and we had dinner nearby. He drove me back the next day for my car.

"I thought you'd eventually cross that line," said Hardye. "And . . . still getting UTIs?"

"Yep."

"I'm so happy for you." She'd known all along. Like Freud said, Eros and Thanatos are inextricably linked.

Scans stable, I texted when I got the results on my way home.

Wonderful news!!! Love you.

That was the last time I heard from Angel Moel.

I sent Hardye an email on February 6, 2023. Nada. So I breathed a sigh of relief when I saw her name in my inbox on February 16.

"Hey, wanted to check in," the subject line read, a continuation of the thread I'd started ten days prior.

"This is Don, Hardye's husband. Sadly, Hardye passed away at home last Thursday. I know she enjoyed knowing and talking with you."

A subsequent email let me know there had been a memorial. I wasn't invited—I hadn't expected to be. Her life was richly populated, and we were . . . what were we? We'd crossed the line beyond mentor-mentee, but we'd never split a restaurant check much less a vacation time-share rental.

I was grateful my own mother wasn't alive when I was diagnosed; it would have killed her. My mother didn't have the instinct or the inclination of a Demeter. In the months before her death, though her love for me was never in question, she confided that she'd never been keen on child-rearing, something that surprised me not at all. She preferred travel. Also antiquing. Volunteering as a docent in art museums. Hard pretzels. Salted nuts. The gravel-shoveling sound as she spooned Taster's Choice instant coffee crystals into hot water. Long, hard crusted baguettes. There, we had something in common.

Hardye had modeled living with gusto while facing mortality. She had a wickedly dark sense of humor. She'd demonstrated determination and dignity in her dying. Hardye was a mother; she was motherly, but she had the detachment to be the hardy mole that I needed.

How do you mourn someone you've never met in person, but who has played an essential role in your survival? I spent a week sitting shiva, giving in to the despair over losing her, and the desperation I felt for my plight, but I couldn't shake my grief. Hardye had put her own feelings aside to champion someone she'd never met. Or maybe, cheering me on was a strategy for processing her feelings? I'd have to follow her lead, except hopefully not the death part.

"If thoughts and prayers have been requested, then I won't be a good match," I wrote on my application to be an Imerman Angel, "but if you've got someone who would like reassurance that everything doesn't happen for a reason, I'm ready for my wings."

I had been angeling a few months with my assigned mentee when I was contacted by Angel Central. Would I be open to taking on an additional match? An additional match? Did that mean that Hardye had numerous assignments? I'd assumed that I was her only charge. Had Hardye ministered to an army of acolytes? Were they all as convinced of their special connection? Did I want to know the answer to that question?

I will never know, because instead of querying Mr. Moel or Angel Central, I decided that until I double died, I'd double down. I added that second mentee, and another, and a few more.

Hardye's reluctance to discuss her worries is understandable to me now. I don't do that with my mentees. Hardye, I'm sure, had her own angel as well.

Angel upper management reminds us in the Angel Rules of Engagement that "a match might last for a lifetime or be as fleeting as a phone call." Some of my matches reached out only once; others talk and text every week. We are spread across the globe. Some I've yet to meet. Others have been houseguests while on vacation or in town to see doctors. The advocacy community Hardye introduced me to provides the strength, hope, and experience I'd desperately craved. None of the early care teams had informed me of their existence, and they have become another chosen family. The proximity to loss is a given.

What was the role angels are supposed to play in our lives, anyway? During my Reform Jewish Sunday school classes in the 1970s, we didn't learn about angels, but we did watch *Charlie's Angels* religiously. In that series, angels selflessly carried out tasks to help humans in need; they also had great hair.

Hardye set the bar high on all accounts, and she did it while rocking that golden halo.

Flowers for Algernon

We were terrible and we were magnificent.

If you were to ask, Jessica, Neena, and I would each recount different versions of our time together, but we agree on that much. For one brief, shining moment, we showed promise. But by the end, we were worse than when we started, and in that failure, Flowers for Algernon was a complete success.

A year into treatment, I was Zooming regularly with my East Coast friends, Jessica and Neena. It was the pandemic, and everyone had something to unpack. Neena's two high-schoolers were home, and Jessica had her children, who'd been in college, back at home too.

Despite growing up a handful of miles from each other in Miami, Neena and I hadn't attended the same schools, so our paths never crossed until we met on a local synagogue-sponsored trip to Israel in ninth grade. We toured historic sites, worked the fruit trees, and weeded cotton for the kibbutzim, something that might now be considered unpaid labor, but it was a different time.

A shared love of reading led me to suspect that she and I were kindred spirits, and the instinct proved correct. We've built a friendship of forty-five years. We followed similar career paths, working in theater and television, and have collaborated numerous times. Remembering Joyce, her mother, of whom I was fond, has been made even more precious since her passing. For years, I repeated the story of how Neena was a "goody-goody," the only one of us who wore the red beanie we were instructed to don for easier spotting in the bustling markets of Jerusalem. I'd seen this anecdote as a funny childhood illustration of a trait you wouldn't associate with nonconformist Neena. Only after decades of hearing me trot out this tale did she tell me she felt it characterized her in a way she didn't appreciate. I retired that story and am resurrecting it now as a testament to Neena's graciousness in forgiving my insensitivity, how memory is a trickster, and how I'm an idiot. A few years back, I found one of the few pictures I still have from the trip. Guess which one of us is the "goody-goody" wearing the red beanie?

Jessica and I met in our twenties, workshopping one of Neena's plays. I was predisposed to love her on Neena's recommendation alone, but you can't not love Jessica. "But why? Why does everyone love Jessica and I'm an acquired taste?" I once asked my ex. "Jessica radiates warmth," he said. "Even your edges have edges."

When Ezra was a teenager, he stayed with Jessica's family in New York for a few days. "Mom, Jessica is a better mother than you," he told me upon his return. Repeatedly.

At first, it irked me. But eventually it became a running joke in my family. "Yes, Ezra," I'd sigh. "I know. Jessica is a better mother than me." To the surprise of no one, she became a Broadway staple, praised for her "warm maternal heart," as one *New York Times* review put it.

The Zooms with Neena and Jessica had a different quality than the breezy backyard coffee klatches with Sarah and Jill. Our time was broken up with badminton, dogs chasing squirrels, and savoring the gluten-free bread pudding and other celiac-friendly desserts I scoured Los Angeles to find for Sarah. Zoom has a way of narrowing space and perspective. For every hour we'd spend together, I'd feel so wrung out emotionally, I'd need two to recover. I started brainstorming ideas. What pursuit could be shared online? At that time, friends were hosting game nights and book clubs, and my sister and I were doing online yoga classes, blowing air-kisses across the continent between downward-facing dogs. Neena had learned no-knead baking online, but mastery of a skill was the furthest thing from my mind. I was already adapting to life in treatment. Wasn't that enough?

"How about ukulele lessons?"

I wanted to do something that had a low barrier to entry. I assumed that we all had ukes. Every teenager in America seemed to have taken up the ukelele during the pandemic. I'd bought one for Ezra, and naturally ended up with it after he bucked the trend. Sure enough, Neena had one "just sitting there, looking cute," as did Jess.

I'm sure I said that we should pledge to never practice, and, in fact, to keep it purely recreational, our not improving should be an intention. They're both adamant that they'd have dismissed the notion out of hand. Neena was certain that anyone could learn to play the uke. She'd taken guitar lessons in high school and felt pretty good about her strum. Jessica recalls thinking, "I will learn the uke, and someday, when I'm asked to play one for a role, I will be ready."

Sara—with no *H*, a singer-songwriter and musician who'd taught a variety of instruments to many kids in our community, agreed to teach us. We set a regular weekly time (though which night of the week, none of us can recall without referring to our calendars).

In another era, it would have turned into one of Bob Mankoff's iconic *New Yorker* cartoons: "How about never? Does never work for you?" But in the pandemic everyone had time.

Now I had Sunday hangs with Sarah and Jill and uke seshes with Neena, Jessica, and Sara. Two Stammtisches. Two anchors to keep me from capsizing.

During our first sessions, Sara demonstrated finger placement for chords. The goal of playing together thwarted by Zoom lag, we took turns strumming through progressions. Next, Sara taught us "You Are My Sunshine" and other songs you would pick for children. Which seemed appropriate.

We played with such guilelessness and concentration, directing our background anxieties onto the two inches of fretboard. Sara beamed at us like a proud parent. We cheered each other on as if encouraging children sounding out words for the first time.

It wasn't a stated goal, but we were cultivating what psychologist Mihaly Csikszentmihalyi calls a flow state, a total absorption produced while engaged in high levels of concentration, like when playing a sport, practicing a musical instrument, or performing brain surgery. In *Flow: The Psychology of Happiness*, he argues that while we might assume that rest produces happiness, intensely focused activity produces a more durable gladness. Our Zooms were examples: wholly invigorating.

Singing hadn't been part of the plan, but I found myself quietly repeating chord names: G-G-G . . . A-A-A . . . E-E-E . . . Eventually, we were strumming and humming along. As we graduated to "This Land Is Your Land," a personal favorite, I tentatively began singing along. Jessica and Neena followed suit. Or had they initiated the singing? Who can recall?

Sara was convinced that we were improving. She floated the idea of a concert. I tried to explain I wasn't keen on singing in public—we all did—but when Sara opened her mouth to sing, it was like warm honey being poured over warm honey, and she couldn't grasp why anyone wouldn't want to be working toward a goal and an audience.

When I say no one wants to hear me sing, I'm not being modest. I can read music thanks to childhood violin lessons, and I can hit notes, but my singing is the equivalent of eating 99 percent cacao: technically chocolate, but without any of chocolate's rich pleasure.

Something shifted with the introduction of "Rainbow Connection."

I'm sure it was Neena, but she says it was Sara who suggested it to the group. Neena says she's "just not that into" Kermit the Frog, whose version in the 1979 *Muppet Movie* introduced the song to the world. This made me question our friendship. If you don't feel something when Kermit croons and strums that banjo, a wellness check might be in order.

Kermit sings with disarming directness, free of operatic embellishments. He offers no cloying expressions designed to produce an emotional response, a limitation of the hard edges of his puppet face. He's just a simple puppet frog with a simple puppet frog voice. "Kermit has 'found his voice,'" as Jessica explained it. When she accepted the role of Golde in the 2016 Broadway production of *Fiddler on the Roof*, she'd never sung professionally. Worried about underserving the classic, she enlisted a coach to "find her voice," as he put it. He'd had her work on songs she already had deep connections to, not the *Fiddler* score, so she could take her authentic experience into the performance. She was able to occupy the stage with authority and found a voice that fit her and the character.

Jessica describes her voice as having a "searching quality . . . searching for the note, searching for answers, searching for the reason that I'm singing."

Neena describes her voice with a story. In high school, she was cast in the chorus of the musical *Paint Your Wagon*. The director took her aside and said, "You don't need to sing; you can just mouth the words."

"The thing is, when I'm singing, I hear it in my head and it sounds pretty good," Neena told us. "But as the sound travels through the air, it turns into the opposite of what I'm hearing." My heart swelled to see Neena, not one for performing, singing without apology, a quality distinctive in her writing too.

I was that teenager who sang the Joni Mitchell songbook in a lilting soprano in my bedroom. But even that feeble facsimile of Joni wasn't available to me now. I'd thought lung cancer was the gift of a two-pack-a-day habit, but ironically, the strain on my vocal cords from increased coughing, another side effect of the medication, has meant lung cancer gave me a two-pack-a-day husky rasp. At times, I couldn't recognize my own voice as I was speaking.

Neena said I was channeling something like what is needed to sing Kurt Weill's discordant and atonal songs in Brecht's plays: "an intentional, alienating flatness." I prefer to characterize it as the plaintive howl of a wounded animal. But who am I to argue with Kurt Weill or Neena? You say atonal flatness, I say plaintive howl; either way, I conjured a new voice for this second life, and a time machine.

Now our ukes became an afterthought. We were barely paying attention to our playing, except for Neena, who really did have a good strum. Sara would show up with a quizzical, bemused expression, but eventually, after giving up on the concert idea, she politely recused herself.

We giddily traded songs like teenagers at a sleepover. And in another unmistakable sign that we'd turned the clock back, I entertained my ultimate teenage fantasy. I was sure I possessed some undiscovered genius which, conveniently, required zero effort on my part. I would wake up one day playing Bach or speaking fluent Portuguese.

Here was my internal monologue during our sessions:

I'm one of the greatest undiscovered singers in the world. When I die, I'll leave instructions for Neena and Jess to have this recording played and people will fall over in their seats at the memorial, wailing with grief unleashed by my vocal stylings. "She really found her voice," they'll say . . . Or: I will be discovered at sixty; the profile in an obscure online theater rag will read: Terminally ill cancer patient and actress is slated for Broadway debut in SOME SHOW WRITTEN FOR ME *featuring her devastating rendition of "Rainbow Connection." "Thank God Annabelle Gurwitch got cancer, or we'd never have known of her unsung talent," a reviewer will write. I will go on* The Voice. *I will get Simon Cowell's golden buzzer. They love the dying!*

We went full-on teenage when we decided "our band" needed a name. Flowers for Algernon was our top pick, though none of us can remember who thought it up. The novel by Daniel Keyes was required middle school reading in the 1970s. It tells the story of Charlie, who has a limited IQ, and is subjected, along with a white lab rat named Algernon, to an experimental brain surgery that transforms them both into geniuses. Only: The procedure is effective for a limited amount of time. Charlie witnesses the rat's regression knowing that he will lose his newly acquired intelligence.

Our uke group was living out the premise of this novel. I was also on a medication that would stop working, but no one mentioned that.

Neena's son, Dashiell, designed our band T-shirts: a ukulele (just sitting there, looking cute) on a patch of grass. A white rat rests on the fretboard, kicking back, smiling, stretched out as if on a chaise longue. Three flowers decorate the uke, symbolizing the three of us: a daisy, a peony, and a violet. I chose a daisy, the most unassuming of flowers, but neither Neena nor Jessica remembers which flower represents them. Both love peonies, but Neena might have picked the violet because it was her mother's favorite, and Jessica often feels like a "shrinking violet" but suspects she might have selected the peony as a self-suggestion to have more authority.

How and why Flowers for Algernon disbanded wasn't fraught or dramatic. As things began opening up, schedules got busier, we canceled, rescheduled, canceled again, rescheduled with high hopes and exclamation marks, but then one day we stopped trying.

"The day Covid ends will be the best day of my life," Dashiell said to Neena, but it didn't really end. The strain just weakened. Our need for the seshes waned as well, until "How about never, does never sound good to you?" became a reality.

None of us have picked up a uke since. Jessica says if the day comes when she's asked if she plays, "I will not be raising my hand in the affirmative." Neena says that our low-stakes noodling cemented our group dynamic. We all agree that it was a kind of balm in Gilead, the best kind of time travel imaginable, and wildly liberating. Jessica puts it this way: "We typically think of the barometer of intimacy as having shared our most private thoughts, but this was something more primal."

Some Stammtisches serve a purpose within particular time frames. Despite best efforts, those standing weekly lunch dates with coworkers are impossible to resurrect when you're no longer working together. The Sunday Friends continue to meet with few interruptions. We switched to Zoom for six months in 2023 when Jill took a sabbatical from teaching to complete a master's degree in Costa Rica. Flowers for Algernon concluded and we never got those T-shirts made, but if one of us shows up in a blouse that we all like, we'll surprise each other by buying it for the others. This is a form of "twinning," a term applied to adolescent girls mirroring each other in dress as a form of bonding, though in this case it's more of a "throupling." In 2025, all of us were equally eager to read Henry Alford's Joni Mitchell biography. I made sure to attend a reading and get three copies inscribed to the Flowers.

I like to imagine that we are still serenading each other in some cyberspace cloud: lighting up a dark fiber-optic cable in Silicon Valley. This data could provide definitive proof of what we sang, when we sang it, and how it sounded, but these videos must never be viewed, because the most accurate accounting of that time is the sacred and silly memory we each hold, each distinct version being the one that is most true.

There's Magic in the Air

It was a temperate seventy-two degrees. The sun lit up the Pacific Ocean in glittery flashes and cotton candy clouds puffed across a perfect blue sky as I chugged north on a highway that clings to the edge of the continent.

I clocked the Malibu Wellness Expert; Daily Calm Wellness; the Wellness Club; the Ranch Wellness Center; SoulSpace Healing and Wellness; Zuma Wellness; Cure Wellness; One Health Wellness; Sukha Wellness Institute; Avalon Integrative Wellness; White Chakra (which didn't have the words *wellness* or *health* in the name, but they were implied); All's Well That Ends Well Wellness (I might have made that one up); Malibu Holistic; Malibu Healing; Mandala Healing; Integral Healing; Iyashi Wellness; Plant Wellness; Well, Well, Well, Wellness (I definitely made that one up); and then, my destination: the Quantum 360 wellness center.

In the center's waiting room, a wall sign directed me to surrender my phone for safekeeping during my visit as protection from harmful 5G radiation. The receptionist's phone was visibly resting on his lap, so I decided to take my chances.

He ushered me through a spacious room furnished with two banks of black leather La-Z-Boy recliners overlooking the kind of panoramic ocean view normally reserved for film studio heads and the surviving members of the Beach Boys. Two or three clients were chillaxing in their chairs, each was holding an electronic gadget resembling a Lite-Brite. The classic 1970s kid's toy was a screen onto which small colored bulbs could be manipulated into images or swirly abstract patterns that perfectly prepared us for another staple of 1970s adolescence: tripping on acid. One client had a green drink in hand. We made our way to a glass cubicle for my intake consultation with the proprietor of Q360.

I listened intently as the proprietor explained how he could harness the quantum field's regenerative properties and reinstate the optimal blueprint of my biofield. The apparatuses at the club used cutting-edge technology calibrated to repair damaged DNA through tuning in to 528 Hz frequency, sometimes referred to as "the universal healing tone." Also available for sale were "grounding" bags of Tesla rock nuggets, named for the inventor Nikola Tesla, that purportedly could protect me from that pesky 5G radiation.

The proprietor didn't have a degree in physics, but he did have a jawline you could cut yourself on, along with piercing blue eyes almost identical to the cerulean hue of the Pacific. I dutifully listened and diligently scribbled notes: Something that sounds like interconnectedness! Resonant frequencies! Or did he say resurrection infrequently? Two thoughts occurred simultaneously: There are worse places you could find yourself on a Wednesday morning, and it's possible that the person sitting opposite you is genuinely convinced of the credibility of what he's peddling, because people subscribe in the flat-Earth theory. Don't ask him if the Earth is flat or about the "activated crystal" on his desk, also available for a princely sum. You don't want to know the answer.

I was in Malibu because a friend had texted that she knew "a guy with an energy machine and he's had great results with curing diseases in his garage in Topanga." Topanga Canyon is one of the few remaining hippie enclaves in Southern California, a tangle of dirt roads and dusty hiking paths where Native American dream catchers hanging from rearview mirrors are as commonplace as writers tapping out screenplays in West Hollywood cafés.

When I didn't respond to her initial text, she pinged me a few months later to ask if I'd connected with Topanga Guy. By then, I'd forgotten the context and, being single, thought she was referring to a possible date. "I wouldn't want to date a guy with an energy machine in his garage, so why would I entrust this dude with my life?" was what I wanted to text. But I was just worn down by the crush of recommendations I'd received.

A short residency in Cancerland gave me an unwelcome wagon gift: an ever-present nagging suspicion that if I didn't at least *try* the outlandish cure, I wasn't doing everything I could. When I called to schedule, I learned that Topanga Guy had recently married one of Charlie Sheen's ex-wives and upgraded from his garage to the swanky Herman Miller–bedecked office suite.

I want to believe! That was the tagline for the TV series *The X-Files*. And I wanted to believe that the proprietor was the self-taught scientific savant he claimed to be and that this "resonant light" therapy might be something more than colorful kid's play. It sounded so . . . science-y. The recommendation was just one in a potluck of magical thinking, ancient rituals, and speculative remedies that came my way:

Juicing: If you care anything at all about your health, you need to start juicing.

Turmeric: Add it to everything you eat, even ice cream.

Turmeric: Don't touch the stuff.

Who haven't you forgiven? Forgiveness is essential in curing cancer.

You should let my Yoruba priest pray over you. I trust him more than I do Western medicine.

Stop listening to the news and put yourself in a bubble of kitten and puppy videos.

I don't understand why you're not juicing! It's the one thing you can control and it's so simple!

Juicing is the gateway to wellness woo-woo. Juice acolytes claim benefits ranging from improved IQ to increased longevity. Its anti-cancer properties are so often touted that when I wrote in *The New York Times* that I'd been given a juicer as a present after being diagnosed, dozens of readers sent photos of abandoned juicers they'd also received. Juicers are the Waterford crystal bowls for the newly diagnosed.

I like juice as much as anyone. So when my juicer arrived, I hastily unboxed it. It was a super-sleek model, almost sculptural, seamlessly smooth and bullet-shaped, like Jeff Koons's idea of a sex toy for Amazonian women.

I considered the steps I'd need to take to make juice.

I'd need to have vegetables on hand. This was during a Covid lockdown, and I wasn't doing much shopping, not to mention that the vegetables considered the most potent elixirs are best ordered in a farm delivery box, which sounded expensive. Also, anxiety making. What to get and how much of it? I've never managed to introduce that much organization into my shopping routine, because I'm never sure whether I should order for a day or for a week. I'd also have to make space in my refrigerator, which might mean chucking the prepared foods that were sustaining me because cooking took too much effort.

With the medication making my digestive system unpredictable, sometimes I needed binding foods, like bananas, and others more fibrous vegetables, like celery. If I went too far in either direction, I could be out of commission all day. And if I didn't make the juice, I'd be throwing away food and adding to the local landfills. Also, since I had to take a nap after making my morning coffee, I'd need to do that, make the juice, and I'd need another nap after the exertion of making the juice. Then I'd need to clean the machine and the juicing area, after which I'd need another nap. I could probably, possibly, fingers crossed, get it all done by bedtime. After a week of feeling guilty every time I caught sight of the awe-inspiring exemplar of culinary engineering and daily reminder of my failure to juice, I disassembled it. Juicing is a fantastic activity for the really healthy.

I also had empirical, if anecdotal, evidence that ran counter to the healing properties of juicing. Frank, who'd recommended my oncologist, had been a juicing evangelist. I'd spoken with him only once, but during that call, he'd told me that his doting wife had prepared juice for him every single day since his diagnosis. But he'd still succumbed to the disease. Maybe he hadn't juiced enough? Maybe he hadn't been drinking the right juice? Maybe he hadn't juiced at the right time of day? Maybe Frank used the wrong kind of juicer? The Gerson Institute, the center of the juicing universe, alleges that you can derail the juice's curative powers by using the wrong device (the machine they endorse will run you over two thousand dollars). This line of questioning can eat away at your resolve while convincing you that if an unproven wellness fad doesn't work, it's entirely your fault.

Any way you slice it, squeeze it, or strain it, you can't outrun the creep of quackery.

Even the most informed of my fellow travelers weren't immune to attempts to game the system. Although the guidelines of our Facebook patient chat room stipulate that we share only vetted information and peer-reviewed science, at least once a month a member will post a long list of speculative supplements they swear by or a link to a website run by a survivor of some life-threatening condition who has developed their own protocol.

If the average person in treatment for cancer whimsically adds "cancer" as a prefix to words—we reside in Cancerland, we have cancerversaries; we cancer people can't get enough of cancer humor—peddlers of supplements love to invoke the word "protocol."

It was on Facebook that I first learned about fenbendazole, an over-the-counter dog dewormer some members were taking. This might seem too far-fetched to take seriously if we hadn't been through a pandemic during which the FDA had to tweet on August 21, 2021, "You're not a horse. You're not a cow. Seriously, y'all, stop it" to drive home the point that the antiparasitic ivermectin, wasn't indicated for treating Covid.

The trail started with a link that had been posted to one of the most popular alternative cure sites: ChrisBeatCancer.com.

Chris Wark is adorbs. He looks a lot like the actor Ryan Reynolds—slim, boyishly handsome, nerdy and relatable—only Wark radiates sincerity whereas Reynolds can register on the smarmy side. Once upon a time, Chris Wark had surgery for colon cancer but opted out of chemo, a decision that he claims should have killed him. However, according to the numerous doctors who have tried to correct this narrative through accurate reportage, his chances of survival without chemo were closer to 64 percent.

The home page of his website features an eleven-minute video that Wark touts as containing "everything a cancer patient needs to know." Only it's not everything because Wark has protocols and modules to sell you. Modules are almost as popular as protocols in the alternative-cure culture lexicon. The modules include books, coaching, course guides, videos, audio recordings, and monthly group sessions online. The online coaching program includes support group access, which he tells us is "worth the cost of the course itself," without telling us that there are a myriad of online support groups and educational seminars with medical experts available for free.

One of his books provides recipes for beating cancer; the next is a guide for beating cancer daily (in case you've only been beating cancer on a quarterly basis); the third is his personal testament to how he beat cancer. There's an apple and a carrot on the cover because—shockingly—juicing is part of his regimen.

Wark also interviews like-minded survivors and naturopath types who peddle their own protocol. And you've got to give it to this community of self-healers—they've got esprit de corps. Wark's interviewees include Joe Tippens, a lung cancer survivor who claims he was cured by fenbendazole.

Like Wark, Tippens bailed out of the traditional medical system and claims to have cured himself. Tippens participated in a trial at MD Anderson for a biomarker targeted therapy that has produced the closest thing to a cure out there, but that's a detail he often neglects to mention in his interviews.

A 2019 feature on Tippens that aired on a South Korean TV station (lung cancer is rampant in Asian countries) garnered millions of views on YouTube. Kim Chul-min, a popular Korean comedian and singer who'd been diagnosed, was one of those viewers. Chul-min began blogging about how fenbendazole "eased his pain and improved blood tests." Thousands of South Koreans followed his lead. Oncologists began noticing that, in addition to not curing cancer, the drug had adverse side effects, like severe liver damage. Soon they were making TV appearances in South Korea urging people *not* to take the dewormer. On his deathbed in a hospital in Seoul in 2021, Chul-min recorded an interview disavowing the dewormer. And yet, fenbendazole sales continue to see spikes.

A swirl of conspiracy narratives and prosperity gospel is braided through the alternate-cure world that plays on us folks already made vulnerable by our medical conditions. "Is it God's will for you to have cancer?" is the title of one of the courses Wark offers. Both Tippens and Wark appear on podcasts and at events with religious associations.

The supplement industry both sows and capitalizes on a kind of distrust in governments and large institutions that has long fueled American libertarianism. Tippens has shared his story on the Joe Rogan podcast and it can't be a coincidence that Joe Rogan's and Alex Jones's financial empires were built on nutritional supplement sales.

What Big Pharma doesn't want you to know is a slogan that accompanies many of the sales pitches. The proprietor of the Q360 wellness center has been quoted as saying, "Everything you've been taught about how diseases process and stuff works is not true." And who hasn't had a soul-sucking experience with any of the Bigs? I've lost hours of my life on the phone feeling unheard, trying to reach human schedulers or transfer records. For $175, Chris Wark will spend two hours listening to you. Try finding a doctor who can afford to do that.

If you unpack the worldwide cabal designed by the powerful to keep real cures from us poor disease-ridden peasants, that conspiracy assumes Big Pharma doesn't want relatively inexpensive cures to be proven effective because they can't make money on them. While it's true that funding for studies that could confirm the value of supplements and even basic nutrition is woefully inadequate, if carrots could be shown to cure cancer, you can bet Big Pharma would be in the prescription carrot business. And to be wary of Big Pharma and not Big Wellness seems misguided. "The Global Wellness Industry Is Now Worth 6.3 Trillion" was a headline story Bloomberg published in November 2024, describing the wellness-industrial complex as being larger than the pharmaceutical industry.

But could it really hurt to spend time in a La-Z-Boy facing the ocean, sipping green drinks, and visualizing healing my body?

I'd done time in that world. In my twenties, I floated between healers, psychics, and naturopaths, a closed loop for which this kind of ministering was normalized. We were devout followers of Louise Hay, author of *You Can Heal Your Life*, a *The Secret*–style New Age self-actualization manifesto, which is simply repurposed old-world mysticism. A central component of Hay's message was that diseases and illness were caused by self-loathing and negative thought patterns.

When friends "manifested" AIDS, we blamed ourselves for our failure to heal our friends who blamed themselves for failing to think positively enough. After the death of the friend who'd been the most invested in Hay's theories, I became allergic to magical thinking and all things unproven through peer-reviewed scientific methodology, but that was in the *before times*, and the equipment at the Center looked so shiny and new.

Hay's writing includes detailed explanations of diseases' connections to organs and systems in the body: Cellulite was "stored anger," while lung cancer was "grief stored in the lungs." So when the proprietor of the Q360 wellness center trained his baby blues on me on that sunny afternoon in Malibu and said, "Diseases are caused by negative thinking; your lung cancer indicates that you're harboring toxic levels of grief," I stood up, shaken out of my intimidating language stupor, and said, "No, that's not true," although I was experiencing grief, the grief of knowing that I could never get back the time or the three hundred and sixty dollars I paid for that consultation.

I marched out on wobbly legs. My body carried me, but my brain was still bargaining. Should I stay and try it out just to be able to disprove it myself, or, you know, just in case . . . wasn't Viagra originally indicated for heart disease?

Since the day I came forward, many patients have sought my advice. When Elina called, I listened to her juicing regimen, nodding along silently and trying to be supportive. But then she said she'd started treatment at a clinic in Malibu.

"Oh, no," I said. "Not Denise Richards's (soon-to-be ex-) husband's clinic?"

"At least I'm doing something."

I wanted to say: Doing something, when that something is meaningless, it isn't something, it's nothing. I wanted to quote soul singer Billy Preston: "Nothing from nothing leaves nothing." I wanted to remind her that if Steve Jobs had searched extensively and still couldn't find an alternative cure, then what hope do the rest of us have?

But I didn't. I knew that she knew that already. She'd gotten to that "for as long as we can" place in her treatment.

In November 2024, Elina's husband filed a lawsuit against Aaron Phypers and the Q360 wellness center. On an episode of *The Real Housewives of Beverly Hills*, a show in which Phypers and Richards appeared, he'd claimed, "I remove blocks, discord, information."

And money, he removes money. He forgot to say that. He'd told Elina and her husband that his stem cell treatment had a 98 percent success rate and if it didn't work, he'd refund half the cost. They'd shelled out $126,000. Elina passed in May 2024.

I wish I could report that my journey to the center of the wellness world was my only flirtation with magical mumbo jumbo, but I also allowed myself to be talked into IV vitamin therapy. A friend was adamant about how much it had improved her recovery from Covid, and when I was experiencing a Covid rebound, I thought it would be less exhausting to just pony up for an infusion at a local med spa than to explain one more time how an oncologist had given me a detailed explanation as to why it was a waste of my time and money.

I was sitting in the spa's storefront waiting room, filling out my intake form, when I spotted Jeremy's kids passing by on the sidewalk. I jumped up and hid behind a column, embarrassed to be caught partaking of something I regularly rail against. During the next few hours after the infusion and before peeing out an ungodly amount of very expensive urine since your body can't absorb that amount of vitamins that quickly, I felt energized and my skin was visibly plumped, which, as I understand it, was simply an indication that I'd been dehydrated. But I knew there was no long-term health benefit. I'd done the research.

"I give up," I sighed after Ezra got a job at a popular juice bar. Was the universe trying to tell me something? I slunk into the joint. "What's your most nutritious green juice? Should I have the "Zeus" with ginger and watercress, or "Eternal Life" with turmeric and Himalayan shilajit?

He didn't hesitate. "'Eternal Life" sucks ass, Mom, you don't want that. Here's what you want, a Greek coffee. It's got dates, bananas, cold-pressed coffee, figs, cardamom, and cacao."

I don't know if a Greek coffee is healthy by any measurable standard, and it doesn't cure worms in canines or humans, but that combination of ingredients makes me glowy, gives me sugar and caffeine-powered energy. And it tastes even better when someone else makes it for me, especially my son.

Still, if you ever hear that I've hung a shingle for Annabelle's Greek Coffee Cure with Turmeric, or find yourself in some sun-splashed Malibu office and notice that I'm one of the clients receiving realigning resonant rays of light, please don't be surprised or disappointed. I haven't gotten the "for as long as we can" call like Elina, not yet. I haven't cycled through a dozen lines of treatment, and I don't know what lengths I'll go to when that day comes.

Also, can I interest you in a juicer? Never used, nearly new. I've got big medical bills, so I'm letting it go for a good price. I'll let you have it for a cool million.

I'm with the Band

It was 11 p.m. and I was staring down an empty suitcase. I was scheduled to catch a 7 a.m. flight from LAX to Heathrow, and hadn't begun packing because even an hour earlier it had seemed unlikely that this trip would materialize. I had no clear picture of where I was going or what I'd be doing once I got there.

Over dinner and a bottle of mid-priced merlot with Jeremy three months prior, he'd proposed that I join him on a whirlwind European jaunt. We'd go to London, Amsterdam, Prague, the Netherlands, and Paris.

I had never turned down a chance to travel, not since that semester as an undergraduate studying art history and theater in London. I'd fallen hard for Turner and Gainsborough and those Pre-Raphealite posers. The luminosity of their subjects' skin, the drama and majesty their thick paint lent to those downs and wolds. My polyester, Lunchables suburban American childhood seemed flimsy by comparison. Annabelle Gurwitch . . . ugh. So unpoetic. *Annabelle Turner . . . Annabelle Gainsborough . . .* I'd inked over and over in looping script in my art history journal, the way other girls in my generation added married surnames in schoolbooks. At the close of the semester, I Eurail-passed it across the continent armed with my older sister's dog-eared copy of *Europe on $10 a Day*. Part of the appeal of a career in the arts was the chance to see the world.

Not to mention, I'd hit a benchmark. Twelve months of stability at the manageable dose.

"What do ya know, it's our cancerversary," my oncologist announced.

"What's the one-year gift?" I'd asked. "Silver, diamonds, a bound leather commemorative copy of my medical records?"

"Now is the time to drink the fine wine," he'd said as he shook my hand. I wasn't sure if his pronouncement was intended as a celebratory toast or a "last call." In either case, a grand tour seemed like exactly what the doctor ordered.

Only, as Jeremy and I drained the last sips of merlot, I learned that this was an invitation to tag along with a heavy metal band that he managed. After a long career as a music executive, he was now trying to "break" a fledgling band.

"This is their first European tour," he said. "To save money, I volunteered to drive the van. You can come along if you'll sell T-shirts."

During one of our first dates, Jeremy had described how booking accommodations for his touring artists was based on two criteria: cheap and clean. Only one of these sounded appealing. "How wonderful for them," I'd said, never imagining that "them" might include me. He'd said that the budget was 115 a night. I was too afraid to inquire if this was euros or dollars. Jeremy used same-day booking services, which portended a kind of unpredictability that seemed terrifyingly fly-by-night to this sixty-year-old.

"I'm in," I'd said, because it sounded like the worst idea imaginable, totally out of my comfort zone, and I'd had several glasses of wine. Besides, the band's last tour had been derailed by Covid, my health might not hold, and our affair might run its course. And I said yes because Paris. Despite its appearance at the top of nearly every bucket list. "I'd like to see Paris before I die," W. C. Fields tells Mae West in *My Little Chickadee*. Moi aussi.

I hadn't been to Paris in two decades. I wanted to stroll cobblestone streets, linger over the Caillebottes at the Musée d'Orsay, wander the Tuileries, and sip espresso at Café de Flore like Samuel Beckett. Jeremy and I would watch the sun set over the Seine, then walk back to our quaint hotel in a scenic arrondissement for an X-rated assignation in our garret, complete with slanted ceiling, toile wallpaper, and a view of the chimney tops of the Left Bank. My fantasy mirrored the set of every production of *La Bohème* ever staged, only with hot water, heat, high-thread-count sheets, and a better ending for me than Mimi. Bogart and Bergman parted ways in *Casablanca*, but they'd always have Paris.

Clearly, the diagnosis was yet more confirmation that the universe doesn't work on anyone's behalf, but it's possible that I'd found favor with a benevolent weather front because plane tickets, which were not in my budget, practically fell into my lap. A film production company offered airline miles in lieu of monetary compensation (it was better for tax purposes) for the rights to an op-ed that chronicled my participation in the assisted suicide of a dear friend, a Francophile who'd had pancreatic cancer. That I'd be using the proceeds from that sale to fund this trip seemed serendipitous. Tagging along with the band would mean my meals and hotels would mostly be covered. If someone had offered the fine wine, I would have accepted. Was cancer making it time to drink the cheap beer?

As our departure date loomed closer, details remained murky. As far as I could glean, during the week I'd join up with the troupe, we'd be on the move with drive times ranging from three to eight hours in the van. This promised a lot of togetherness for people who'd been seeing each other less than three months. We'd never spent twenty-four straight hours in each other's company. We'd never even farted in front of each other.

The miracle drug exacerbated a natural tendency toward gassiness. As a flatulence prophylactic, I'd gone cold turkey on dairy but often had to excuse myself, rushing into the bathroom to turn on the fan, heater, running water, sometimes singing to muffle the sound. Jeremy and I had begun our relationship by taking evening constitutionals together. I'd lag behind, feigning an untied shoelace, waiting until he was just out of range and the wind was just right to unburden myself in the night air. All of this carefully preserved mystery could quickly crumble in such close quarters.

I'd already booked my nonrefundable ticket when Jeremy texted that the band had been invited to play the Pinkpop Festival. This was the European equivalent of Burning Man, but because of the frequency of rainstorms in Landgraaf, the Netherlands, where the three-day fest has been held since 1970, the Pinkpop has a reputation as one of the most popular mud festivals on the continent. Big groups like Imagine Dragons and Metallica had played there, drawing crowds of a hundred thousand fans every year.

Jeremy was elated because the band's appearance could prove a key stepping stone to booking bigger venues and better compensation for the guys down the road. Me, not so much. One of the few places I'd never longed to visit was an outdoor festival. I had close friends who recounted their pilgrimages to Burning Man with whispered reverence. They'd fallen head over barefoot heels in love, reconnected with their soul's purpose, and had their hair braided by roving bands of naked mermaids at the annual eight-day festival in Black Rock City, Nevada. Between the dust, the heat of the day, the cold of the night, and the sheer number of the assembled, just no.

How do you feel about camping on the festival grounds? Jeremy texted. He was having difficulty finding affordable lodgings near the festival. Muddy camping and porta-potties? I'd been googling local spas. Maybe I'd made cancer look too good? Aware of the toll my health had taken on my friends and family, I hadn't mentioned that side effects still flared up. It had been just over a year since the night I'd been dubbed Cancer Mom, and things remained unpredictable.

I'm game for anything as long as that anything includes indoor bathrooms. But can we do something special in Paris? I texted back. It would be our longest stay in one location. We'd be there for two nights, and I'd stay on for an additional night, alone, before heading home while they continued to Germany and parts eastward. A thrift-minded traveler friend had recommended a boutique hotel in Paris that looked a lot like my *La Bohème*–y fantasy, and cost just a bit over the band's maximum budget. If you have to stretch the tour budget for the two of us, I'll contribute, I texted.

I knew little about the band, except that the guys were all twenty-seven. The only thing I knew about heavy metal was that the CIA uses Metallica's "Enter Sandman" as a torture method to extract intel from prisoners.

Jeremy had referred to them only as DPS. From their Instagram I saw that stood for Dead Poet Society. The name is one *s* away from being identical to the 1989 blockbuster *Dead Poets Society*, but the band had nothing to do with the movie so that seemed just stupid.

The profile picture on the band's page featured a close-up of the lead singer screaming into a microphone. There was something compelling about his compactness and charismatic about his anger, which I guessed was very rock 'n' roll. Their bassist had the sort of Eastern European features that told me his people were probably from a neighboring shtetl to my ancestors. He looked sulky, a hallmark of rock 'n' roll. The long-limbed drummer had a gangly goofiness: His *let's party!* vibe was definitely rock 'n' roll. Then there was the guitarist, who with a thick ginger mane and denser beard bore a striking resemblance to the fearsome assassin from *Game of Thrones*, Tormund Giantsbane. Inked on the guitarist's forearm in a bold, blocky black font was the phrase LET IT RATTLE. I was just plain terrified of him.

They'd recently been on an American van tour. Pictured lounging in the vehicle in Huntsville, Alabama, each occupied their own row. That modicum of personal space seemed promising, though the caption spoke to a twentysomething's sense of humor and laissez-faire attitude toward hygiene that I would soon be subjected to. "Guess who farted?"

In another pic, the lead singer, shorts dangling around his ankles, was gripping a plastic water bottle. This caption read: "This will have to do because there's no place to stop and pee." Uh-oh. One of my enduring side effects was that every time I had sex or even thought about sex, I got a UTI. To lessen the threat of those pesky, endless bathroom runs, I could forgo having sex while on the tour, but that didn't seem very rock 'n' roll.

I'd need to prepare for my new career as Merch Girl. My only association with that term was Pamela De Barres, the inspiration for the Penny Lane character in Cameron Crowe's *Almost Famous*. What I was certain of was that "girl" wasn't going to be acceptable. Merch Crone had a certain je-ne-sais-quoi appeal. "Merch sales are the only money the guys will see," Jeremy explained. But no pressure! He suggested I connect with someone named Ella for tips. "She's the best in the biz," he told me.

Ella turned out to be an ebullient woman in her early twenties blessed with a sunny disposition, dazzling smile, and a boundless enthusiasm for hard rock. Qualities that had eluded me even when

I was her age. She'd sold merch for DPS and other favorite bands as well.

"Oh my God, you're getting to travel in the van? I've never gotten to do that."

"Well, I do have to sleep with the manager," I said, attempting to soften the blow.

"You'll want to practice folding. You'll be working under pressure. And get familiar with the band. What's your favorite song?"

I hadn't listened to their music.

The first song I found of theirs was titled ".CoDA," a throbbing assault to the nervous system. In ".CoDA," the lead singer says, "Talk shit, bitch, don't lie, you need me every night, you love me like cocaine." So, he hated women. Still, I was determined not to let them down, because even if I didn't care for their name, faces, song titles, senses of humor, or their music, the only thing I take more seriously than my split-second character assessments is an appreciation of being a struggling artist.

Anyway, how hard could it be to fold a T-shirt? I pulled up a YouTube tutorial courtesy of a young woman who'd "done time at Target." My initial attempts landed somewhere between bulgy and neck-skin crepey, but once I got the hang of it, the folding technique did make the finished product look more attractive, even expensive—something about clean lines?

In the 1990s, when Emily, my writer friend with the handy LISTSERV, was in her twenties, she'd lived in Portland, so there was a 99.9 percent chance she'd dated a guy in a band. "Musicians on the road are moody," she told me when I reached out for advice. "You'll need to take up as little mental space as possible."

Of all the challenges—the close quarters, long drives with limited bathroom access, having never crossed the flatulence line, the menacing angularity of the lead singer's face, the migraine-inducing music, budget meals, threats to my health—that might be my Waterloo. I steeled my resolve and set intentions for the tour. I was going to move their merch. I was going to keep it romantic. I was going to try not to die. All it would take was turning myself into someone completely unrecognizable.

Now it was 11 p.m. and that suitcase wasn't going to pack itself. At 10 p.m., I'd learned that a last-minute scheduling change meant I'd miss their London gig. Or not. I wasn't actually sure. The band had already crossed the pond and was snaking up and down the UK playing club dates, and between the time difference and the odd hours a touring band keeps, I'd been getting truncated, infrequent, and confusing texts about last-minute cancellations and additions to the tour, apparently not uncommon at this level of the industry. Should I still fly into Heathrow? I'm not sure I understand our itinerary? I texted. Thumbs-up emoji. It was 6 a.m. in London.

I'd need to stick to starchy binding foods, travel with a hefty supply of Imodium, and assemble outfits strategically. How do you pack when you want to affect a sartorial European sophistication and remain festively un-muddy? "Cancer is a gift" is one of my most detested phrases, but cancer makes intercontinental packing easier. Over the years, I'd lovingly preserved my *investment pieces*, but if my finery got ruined in the muck it would have had a good run. I threw in two favorite outfits, leaving space for lingerie to wear in Paris, along with the arsenal of supplies I must have at the ready now that my body is like a temperamental automobile that must be coaxed into revving up on a daily basis.

Since the miracle drug can only be procured by navigating a mail-order system requiring Magellan-like skills, I counted out enough pills from a carefully hoarded stockpile to last a month in case I needed to Covid quarantine somewhere in Europe.

I threw in a half-dozen travel-sized sweet-smelling lotions to mask the geriatric scent of medical-grade moisturizer I use to calm the (external) rashes. I could not turn these twenty-seven-year-olds' tour van into an elder transport vehicle. I chucked in such a laughably large supply of lube that it seemed impossible to believe it was intended for one person.

In some cruelly ironic twist, the medication can be effective in the treatment of melanoma, but it also stops the production of melatonin, which raises the specter of developing melanomas. I had to avoid direct contact with sunlight, continually apply sunscreen, wear hats and shawls when it's 103 degrees. "I knew you had cancer but I didn't know you'd become a Bedouin," a friend had said when seeing me in my new vampiric incarnation.

Along with being cancer-y, I was also menopausal and taking hormone replacements, and an antidepressant as a kind of chaser. I'd scored a supply of antibiotics and over-the-counter UTI symptom-relief tablets. I'd begun the painstaking task of parceling them into a Monday–Sunday pill packet but thought better of it. I imagined the look of surprise on Jeremy's face when he registered the colossal level of maintenance involved in my carefully cultivated, unimpacted-by-cancer lifestyle. I'd decided to extend my *need to know* strategy and conceal the meds in pretty fabric jewelry pouches. I stashed some in my carry-on luggage, but on the chance that I got separated from that bag, I deposited a couple more in my purse, and even put a small supply in my pants pocket, in case our plane went down.

Since fatigue could set in at any time, I'd need to down espressos continuously, which might be the only thing I wasn't worried about having access to while traveling in Europe.

When I finally finished packing, I examined my handiwork and said a secular prayer that we wouldn't get searched at any borders, because between the lingerie, lubes, and assortment of pills, I had the suitcase of a sex trafficker.

It was only as the Uber pulled up to my home that I attempted to close my suitcase; it was so overstuffed that I broke the zipper. I was panting as I lugged my new bag up my driveway. I'd picked one with a misaligned wheel, but it was too late to switch again. This unexpected exertion left me so lightheaded that I closed my eyes and my fall-asleep-anytime-anywhere superpower kicked in. I reopened them just in time to see a sign that read FIFTEEN MILES TO ONTARIO AIRPORT. Whew. We were close, which would allow for a leisurely check-in. Except that I was flying from LAX. We'd driven thirty miles in the wrong direction.

"I'm not allowed to change my route unless you change the address in the app!" the driver tells me as we hurled by yet another freeway exit.

"I am app challenged! Obviously. Otherwise, I wouldn't have made the mistake in the first place."

"I am bound to take you to the address on the app."

"Are you saying that if I put Toronto as my destination, you'd have to take me?" I asked this because even though time was of the essence, I am constitutionally unable to resist a rhetorical argument.

"What if my phone died? What if I died?" I'm not proud of this, but I said, "This is a hostage situation!" Somehow, and I can't even remember how I did it, I rerouted us.

An international flight departing from the international terminal makes sense but at LAX nothing makes sense except that Fodors consistently ranks it as the world's most poorly designed airport. I'd gotten off at the wrong terminal. The right terminal was in sight, only there was no pedestrian crosswalk. I'd have to "Serpentine, Sheldon, Serpentine" a soccer field's worth of traffic lanes or circle the outer perimeter of the airport to get to the right one.

A wave of fatigue washed over me. I didn't have the strength to drag the bag or my body that distance. I'd missed my flights to and from New York, and as upsetting as that was, my time was my own. Missing this flight could throw off the band's schedule. Hurling myself into traffic seemed a better option.

Just as I was about to give up, an airport shuttle flashing the word DISABILITY rounded a bend. I stepped out into oncoming traffic, waving my arms and yelling, "I've got cancer." I'd sworn not to play the cancer card after receiving the stink eye from my dermatologist when I'd asked if he gave cancer discounts on Botox. Maybe it was the crying or the twenty-five bucks I slipped the driver, but he took me directly to the terminal, bypassing an elderly man with a walker. I was a terrible person. I'd held an Uber driver hostage and commandeered a disability shuttle, but karma must not exist in this best of all possible worlds, because I made it to the flight on time. Once on the plane, my trusty superpower kicked in, and I slept through the thirteen-hour flight.

After clearing immigration at Heathrow without attracting enough attention to warrant a bag search, I attempted to text, call, email, and even WhatsApp Jeremy to no avail. I'd practiced folding T-shirts but neglected to arrange for international cell service, which, it turned out, my carrier didn't offer anyway.

I'd gotten suckered into a multiyear contract with CREDO, a company that advertises itself to dyed-in-the-wool liberals as a progressive phone company with the tagline "we donate to good causes," which turns out to be code for "we can't afford cell towers." So there I was punching in letters and numbers on my *woke* phone like a monkey with a typewriter trying for Shakespeare.

With Jeremy handling all the logistics, I'd failed even to ask for an itinerary, and we had no plan B in the event our travel plans went awry.

Twenty minutes went by before I noticed a baby-faced, nattily attired young man, suit and hard shoes, standing a few feet from me. He was clutching a sign with a name on it. A private driver waiting for his pickup.

"Might I possibly use your phone? I've just landed, and my boyfriend is supposed to pick me up, but he's not here." He paused. I could see he was taking me in: middle-aged American woman, maybe close in age to his own mother, expectant look, undercurrent of panic in her voice. He placed a hand comfortingly on my shoulder.

"Have you ever actually met him?" he asked. With a sympathetic squeeze, he added, "Are you . . . sure he's coming?" He thought I'd been catfished, and for a minute, I wasn't sure I hadn't been.

The sole detail I'd parsed from our brief discussions was that to save money, we'd be spending the night just outside London at the rambling estate of an eccentric schoolmate of Jeremy's named Potts. I didn't even know the name of the town, just the name Potts.

Just then, Jeremy strolled up. He was wearing what I'd come to recognize as his standard tour wardrobe: flip-flops, a T-shirt, and shorts. The driver relaxed and wished me good luck. No one would catfish in an outfit like that.

I got my first look at the van in the parking lot. Jeremy gallantly slid the door open for me. As if on cue, a half-empty bag of Walkers crisps rolled out onto the asphalt along with the scents of sweat, nicotine, and stale beer. The band had already been touring for ten days and clearly my arrival wasn't seen as reason to freshen up the joint. The vehicle was narrower and half the length of the one I'd seen on their Instagram. The six of us would need to fit into two rows of seating.

Jeremy said with a smile, "Welcome to your home away from home."

Without so much as a glimpse of Trafalgar Square, we hit the M40. "Staying just outside London" turned out to mean in Surrey, a county south of the city. There'd be no time to squeeze in a matinee, much less an evening show, nor visit my former future husbands—my favorite nineteenth-century landscape artists and the Pre-Raphaelite sleeping beauties at the Tate. As we idled in bumper-to-bumper traffic for three hours, I congratulated myself for taking antibiotics in advance to avoid a UTI. *I got this.*

Jeremy's managerial duties included craft services, and he'd planned a route that took us through Guildford to load up on snacks for the road. "And I'll be able to show you where I grew up," he told me.

A sweet, if mystifying, gesture. Who was this stranger whose childhood home I was about to see? We shopped our way down the old high street, charmingly narrow with its tiny storefronts, low-rise, gabled-roof brick buildings dating to the seventeenth century, then stopped in front of an Elizabethan stone cottage with curved gables and dormer windows. He suggested a jaunt on Pilgrims' Way, an ancient Roman track carved through the local woods.

Tramping along the unpaved path beneath a canopy of leafy oaks, we came face-to-face with an impish beardo. He was wearing a suede tunic over green tights and a horned headpiece, and in his hand clutched a rolled-up manuscript. Either I was experiencing a jet-lag-related hallucination or we'd encountered Puck, the spritely woodland fairy in *A Midsummer Night's Dream*. Before I could stop myself, I threw out the first few lines of one of the central character Helena's speeches: a monologue detailing her many jealousies over Hermia, her rival in beauty, social standing, and, well, everything. "I see we have a Helena here," Puck said, as if this happened on a regular basis, and led us to the low proscenium stage set in an almost perfect semicircle of trees, making for a natural bandshell. There was to be a performance that night—in an actual wood, in actual England, less than three hours from actual Shakespeare's birthplace at Stratford-upon-Avon? This was the ultimate bucket-list fantasy of every classically trained actor! Only, we wouldn't be able to stay because we were expected in Surrey for an impromptu high school reunion. My high school reunion wasn't on my bucket list, so Jeremy's certainly wasn't, but no one had consulted me. At any other point in my life, I would have protested, but I was no longer in my normal life bound by normal rules. I'd come up with Shakespeare's words, but now I was speechless. Had I woken up in a sort of midsummer night's dream?

A winding single-lane bordered with dense hawthorn hedgerows, disorientingly mazelike, delivered us to Potts's country estate in Farnham, a hamlet on the River Wey, a tributary of the Thames, nestled in the rolling chalk hills of Southern England. The town had stone buildings dating from the twelfth century, which we wouldn't tour because friends and cousins had already shown up for the soiree. A bunch of reunioners were staying over and we'd be sharing a bathroom with all of them. The band had stayed out late after last night's show in London and were skulking about in the living room. None approached to greet me.

Farnham is the kind of quaint where buildings had names referring to old uses: "the rectory" and "the old printing house." I was itching to say that it was kind of ironic that this home was the original site of "the respiratory hospital," given that I had lung cancer, but I had no idea what, if anything, Jeremy had told his friends.

Since the diagnosis, I hadn't been in any group that wasn't either mourning my impending death or taking some kind of bodily sample. The cough that led to my diagnosis persisted, and all but ensured my becoming a bona fide buzzkill. Coughing during the pandemic, even when masked, was like shouting "Fire!" in a crowded theater. I felt compelled to reassure dining companions, elevator fellows, or airplane seatmates, "It's not Covid, just lung cancer." Now I was playacting the part of band manager's main squeeze, but no one cared, engrossed as they were in regaling me with the childhood exploits of a man I barely knew.

To save money, we weren't going to the Dog and Pheasant, the local sixteenth-century pub. Instead, our host, there really was a Potts, had cooked up an impossibly large lasagna. It looked like every middle school goopy cheesy vat of Italian-flavored dairy that had torn my stomach apart in those years before the phrase "lactose intolerance" infiltrated our conversations. Determined to be that less gassy and easygoing version of myself that didn't actually exist, I made a spontaneous decision: I would eat only bread on the tour. For the good of the group.

I stole Jeremy away to our quarters, the childhood bedroom of Potts's son. As if a reminder of how alien an environment I'd landed in, we enjoyed a brief interlude on top of a glow-in-the-dark bedspread depicting our solar system, hovering just over Saturn. Sex during a high school reunion, though not on my bucket list, is probably on someone's. In doing so, I managed to knock over a delicate porcelain teacup, becoming the sole member of the band's entourage to destroy a piece of property during our stay. Before I closed my eyes at the end of the first day, I'd checked off one goal: Keep the romance going.

The next days were a blur of logistics, with each hour reinforcing my status as the least important person in the van. We pushed toward the biggest booking of the tour, the festival in the Netherlands. "How about we not take the scenic route," no one suggested, but that's what we did, hitting the motorway after dropping the band off at the airport for last-minute booking in Prague. Jeremy's and my schedule demanded strict adherence to time management. In my Wi-Fi void, untethered from work, friends, and family, we pressed north to Harwich, our departure port.

Harwich is a scenic seaside town known for being the launching spot for the *Mayflower*, but we had time only to tour the Tesco petrol station before joining the immigration checkpoint queue. The officers couldn't wrap their heads around what we oldsters, an American and a New Zealander, were doing crossing on a lorry drivers' ferry in a van with the back half boarded up and windows blacked out. They dismantled the drum kit searching for contraband and when they eyed my suitcase—stuffed with lube, lotions, and lingerie—I burst into a nervous giggling fit that culminated in a fart. Loud enough to be heard by everyone present. Our first fart, and of course, it was mine. Luckily, a strong breeze blew in from the channel, and with raised eyebrows we were waved on.

Once aboard, it became clear that the ship was run with all the élan and precision of a floating penal colony. As drivers double-fisted steins of beer in the commissary, we attempted a Kate/Leo embrace on the bow, but, thick with cigarette smoke, the vibe was less *Titanic* than Hells Angels rally. Every few minutes, a three-tone alarm heralded high-pitched instructions over a loudspeaker: *check in on the dormitory level, the cafeteria is closing, lockdown at ten, random body cavity searches will be conducted.*

By 10 p.m., it was a ghost ship. Our cabin was pleasant, just big enough for a bed, and it had a porthole. The bathroom, a paper-thin prefab affair, inches from our bed, afforded no privacy. Thankfully, I'd stuck with the bread-only diet. As a blanket of mist settled over the North Sea, I straddled Jeremy, one foot planted on the floor due to the size of our bed: Sexual encounter on a body of water. Check.

"Wake up will be at five thirty a.m. for breakfast and drive off," the warden announced. *Isn't that funny? We're tourists conforming to a lorry driver's schedule.* Just before I fell asleep, the realization hit me: We were lorry drivers.

The next morning, we disembarked at the Hoek of Holland, a port city in the southwestern corner of the country. We cruised past postcard-perfect fields of tulips, grazing cows, and the occasional windmill, en route to Amsterdam. Only, to save money, we were staying at a pop-up in the burbs, an office building hastily repurposed as an Airbnb during the pandemic. It was clean and cheap, modular, with zero ambience, underwhelming in the sense that you're anticipating a night on the town in Manhattan and discover you're spending the night in an accountant's office in Weehawken.

After dropping our bags, Jeremy set to work. There were guest passes to wrangle, set lists to convey, hotel rooms to reserve. Having spent so little time together, I'd had no idea that he was in charge of details I'd assumed were carried out by support staff. "We should catch a trolley into town and visit Anne Frank's house," I suggested. I offered to take charge of the small window of time. We had an airport run for the band at the crack of dawn. "I'll serve as tour guide and you can keep working."

Half of the Western world knows where the Franks hid, but I never found the Frank House. After an hour of circling, backtracking, and general confusion, I gave up.

Jeremy, nose buried in his phone, didn't appear to notice that I'd begun weeping. It was something of a relief, to not have to explain myself, but on the other hand, it was odd. Was this some iteration of Kiwi sturdiness or British stoicism, stiff upper lip and all that?

Looking over his shoulder, I saw that he—or, I supposed, we—had supply chain problems. Since the pandemic, the preferred merch supplier had gone out of business. T-shirts had been shipped that read DEATH POET SOCIETY, which I preferred to the actual name, Dead Poet Society, but no one consulted me. Jeremy remained calm but was scrambling to locate another vendor. A saying often repeated by one of the meditation teachers whose lectures I'd been listening to popped into my head: "You are the sky; everything that happens is weather." This prompt is intended to help you "gain custody of your mind" and stay present. I repeated that and turned my attention to an awareness of pressing the backs of my legs on the wooden bench and the clicking sounds of bike gears of the passersby. By the time we'd trolleyed back to our office park, I was no longer spinning out. *Look at how late-afternoon light glints off the metal roof of the porta-potty outside the entrance of our hotel.* I knew there'd be porta-potties on this trip.

In the morning, I woke up early to get a jump on downing espressos and ordered a half-dozen pastries before leaving for the airport with Jeremy to pick up the band. I'd win the boys over by embodying the cliché of a Jewish mother: I'd feed them.

At the airport, I could see they were out of sorts, worried over the merch shipment. Also, the guitarist had left his suitcase in Prague and was fuming. I held up the bag of warm croissants and sticky buns. "Oh, great! We're all on diets," the bassist grumbled, but grabbed the bag anyway.

As the least essential and smallest person in the crew, I was assigned to sit on the hump of the front row, squashed between a band member and Jeremy, who was driving. I learned that this was called "riding bitch." I never saw them discuss this, but the band must have been doing some kind of rock, paper, scissoring over who would sit next to me, an assignment that involved our thighs being pressed together, because each time we piled in and out of the van, a different one slid into the front row.

Because of the seating arrangement, I was put in charge of directions. Desperate to earn my keep, I neglected to mention the challenges I'd been having in this arena. My geographical proximity to the lone charger also meant I was now on phone-charging duty, with individual phones being passed to me in rotation. Despite being fundamentally derelict in all things technological, I assumed the role of personal assistant for Jeremy and the guys, who still didn't seem to know my name.

The Dutch countryside flashed by in shapes and shades of greens: Scots pines, flat grassy fields, sloping grassy fields, farmland, more pines, more farms, more fields of green. David Hockney's *Flight to Italy—Swiss Landscape* is a satirical painting of a sedan crammed with British tourists crossing the Alps. Streaks of paint obscure the details of the car, indicating the speed of the vehicle. On one side of the canvas, PARIS is scribbled with an arrow pointing in the direction the vehicle has come from; BERN is printed in the far corner of the other side of the canvas. "That's Switzerland, that was," observes one of the travelers. It is one of my favorite pieces of modern art. You can't help but laugh at his satirical depiction of *just passing through*. I just never wanted to wake up inside it.

We zipped along in hope of arriving with enough time for a solid night of rest before Pinkpop. Local accommodations were out of range of our budget, so we wouldn't be sleeping in the Netherlands. We were gunning it for Belgium, where, in a stroke of luck, Jeremy had secured same-day reservations at a two-hundred-year-old Belgian farmhouse near the border. The inn had a Michelin-starred restaurant. Now *was* the time to drink the fine wine!

If we stuck to our route, we'd make it in time for the last seating, only, that was when the drummer announced something that will surprise no one who frequents music festivals: We should be tripping on 'shrooms.

Along with universal health care and sex workers, psilocybin mushrooms are easily obtained in the Netherlands. Alas, the drummer accidentally entered the address for an outlet in Rotterdam, instead of one on our route. The detour added two hours each way.

Those hours were passed in tense silence, broken only as each time we crossed a country border the guys' phones dinged, signaling additional data time on international plans. We arrived at the farmhouse close to midnight. "We're sorry you missed dinner, but we can serve you some bread," the proprietor offered.

What a treat, bread!

Our host set up a table on a brick patio next to a lily-pad-laced pond, where every frog in the known universe gathered to greet us. It was mating season. We'd just sat down with a pretty good wine under the starry domed sky when our host, almost as ancient as the farmhouse, called it a night.

The guys were staying in a children's dormitory-style room, while Jeremy and I were ushered to an attic room accessible through back staircases and hidden doors. The room had broad wooden floors and a soaring vaulted ceiling. Moonlight streamed through round portholes. An oversize gilded antique mirror was propped against the wall facing the bed, low to the ground. It was artsy, sexy even, and that it was stifling hot and lacked air-conditioning seemed appropriate; we opened the windows to the sound of the frogs croaking in the distance. It was surprisingly close to my *La Bohème* fantasy, only our bathroom appeared not to have a door. I examined the entryway at eye level. I probed the wooden frame with my fingers, searching for a pocket door. I walked in and out of the doorway several times. Had someone slipped me mushrooms? What hotel room has a bathroom without a door? Ever resourceful, Jeremy set off to locate a private bathroom for me. He was successful, only: It was an ancient water closet down a dark hallway with a chain toilet. He'd found me Anne Frank's bathroom.

Also, along with no door, the attic room appeared not to have a connection to a hot water heater. Perhaps it was all in service of treating us to an authentic eighteenth-century farmhouse experience. Or there was a reason this room was available at such short notice.

In the morning, I rose early. Wending my way down one back staircase and then another, I caught sight of our surroundings. We'd arrived so late, I'd been unaware that we'd landed inside a Dutch Old Master's agrarian landscape: Farmland stretched seemingly to the horizon, the big sky cloudless, a Flemish slate gray. A horse grazed in a field just beyond the main house. I leapt down the stairs and rushed into paradise. While everyone else slept, I downed espressos. Soccer goals had been set up in a field adjacent to the frog pond and I kicked a ball from end to end, in hopes of exercising my way to regularity. As I charged up and down the field, a passel of horses trotted over to the wooden fence separating us. I wanted to stay in this Shangri-la, hot water or no, but it was showtime.

The guys were grumpy. Their room was located just above the pond. Randy frogs had kept them awake all night. They were also nervous about the big names that were on the bill—Nile Rodgers, Ziggy Marley, Imagine Dragons. During the two-hour drive, I gave them the silent treatment. Only, no one noticed. I was a background actor in the movie of their lives.

When we pulled into the loading area of the festival, a security guard barked, "You're Stage Five." For a moment, I genuinely panicked, thinking he meant stage 5 in medical terms. But the band was booked on Stage Five, the smallest on the sixty-six-acre fairgrounds. We were instructed to park and as we schlepped the mile to the Siberia of performance spaces, a hard rain began to fall. I was planning to collapse in the band's dressing room, only Stage Five artists didn't merit a private dressing room. Instead, there was a makeshift structure, a tent, barely big enough for the band and the two other acts with whom they were sharing the space. I knew there'd be a tent on this trip! The cramped enclosure had a couple of metal folding chairs and a card table with fewer bottles of water than there were band members and a single open bag of chips.

The only shaded "napping" spot I could locate was a concrete slab under a picnic table next to the tent. At least the rain had slowed to a drizzle. I closed my eyes, my purse serving as a pillow. Just before my I-can-fall-asleep-anywhere superpower kicked in and I drifted off, I heard the lead singer running through the same set of vocal warm-ups I'd been trained to do as an actress. The drummer was tap, tap, tapping on a table inside the tent with his drumsticks. He had been wearing headphones since I'd joined up with them. It hadn't occurred to me that he was listening to rehearse to the tracks they would be playing. Had I underestimated them?

When I awoke, the backstage was bustling with equipment load-in. DPS would be the first act of the first day of the festival. Even I, who knew nothing about touring bands, knew enough to know that wasn't a plum spot. At least the rain had stopped.

The stage, though the smallest, was stadium-sized, commanding a field that could hold thousands. I planted myself backstage in a spot I hoped would be convenient in case anyone needed an errand run or someone to actively ignore. Gazing out over the vast expanse, I saw just one person, a superfan sitting crisscross applesauce in front of the stage. Uh-oh. What would the mood in the van be like if the band bombed here?

I braced myself.

Jeremy, meanwhile, was doing managerial things when he spotted Superfan. He strode onto the stage, pulled off his T-shirt, and, shirtless, swung it over his head and lobbed it to the guy. It was a winning display of generosity, and undoubtedly the most rock 'n' roll thing I had ever witnessed from a senior citizen, having never attended a Rolling Stones concert.

With an hour to go before the show, I set out to do recon at the merch stalls. Throngs of boho festivalistas perused row after row of drapey, flowing shawls and witchy black frocks, clothing I characterized as *things Stevie Nicks might wear.* Couldn't these Rhiannons with their "you can go your own way" getups see they were just as much of a cliché as the countrified casual "coastal grandmas," resplendent with their rough-hewn starched lavender-scented linen in shades of ecru, biscuit, and Sagaponack sand? I shuddered with delight. Still got it! *It* being a streak of split-second judgmental bitchiness. Cancer wasn't going to strip that essential element from my character.

Jeremy and I were standing in the wings when the band took the stage. The stadium was still terrifyingly empty. "Here goes nothing," the bassist said as he slunk past us. This would be my first time seeing them play live. They seemed taller on stage. More cohesive—less distinct disgruntled humans and more of a disgruntled machine. It was so . . . rock 'n' roll?

".CoDA," the song whose first few bars had hit me like an anvil, seemed suddenly sticky. "Talk shit bitch, say you wanna leave, you love me like cocaine." Despite having heard the song all of one time, I sang along and spotted other women singing too. The lead singer had that angry expression I'd clocked on Insta, but he wasn't screaming, he was hitting the high notes, his bell-like voice ringing out. Now the crowd swelled from one to a few hundred to several thousand. Later we would learn that the DJ at Stage Five had been won over by Jeremy's act of generosity and decided to get behind the band. He'd put out the word to the DJs at the other stages to shuck for DPS. A booker for a German festival approached me demanding to know if I was the band's manager. "No, I'm their Merch Girl, but I am sleeping with the manager!"

It was then that the moshing began. I slipped out of the backstage area and waded into—well, maybe not into, but toward the crowd. No one seemed to give a second thought that an *old* was swaying on the outer ring; there was a safe-space vibe, and unlike those male-dominated 1980s mosh pits, this was multigendered. I'd hoped to live long enough to see women bridge the gender pay gap. Alas, I'm not sure I will, but female-friendly mosh pits are, if not one great leap, one small jostle for female kind. I didn't want to push my luck, so when the lead singer vaulted into the pit and crowd-surfed his way across the length of the stage, I made my way backstage.

By the time the band reached the end of their set, the festival crew estimated the crowd at ten thousand strong. "We never do this because it screws with the schedule, but the crowd's demanding an encore," the stage manager announced, dubbing them the breakout stars of the fest and taking photos that would later be splashed across the festival's home page. Jeremy and I hugged each other and jumped up and down with joy, as if celebrating our kid's bar mitzvah.

The band was so elated that it wasn't hard to talk them into a celebratory photo with me, even though none of them had yet addressed me by name. Looking at the image as we pulled onto the motorway, I had two mortifying realizations. One: I'd captured this jubilant moment without noticing the toilet paper stuck to the lead singer's sneaker. Two: The photo showed a crone clutching a starched linen hat, sporting a 70s-style shawl and flouncy black muslin tunic with asymmetrical hemline and raw edgings. I was the embodiment of a Fleetwood Mac festivalista meets coastal grandma.

I'd been "riding bitch" for seven hours when we hit the outskirts of the City of Love. Sandwiched between Jeremy, who was fast asleep, and the lead singer, who had taken the wheel when we crossed the border from the Netherlands into Belgium. It was 1 a.m. Everyone else conked out as Belgium slid into France.

I'd peppered the lead singer with questions about his family, how he was able to channel so much rage so effortlessly on stage, anything to make sure he stayed awake. I'd learned that ".CoDA," which I'd assumed had been his composition, was actually written by an ex-bandmate he'd met at Berklee College of Music and that the band had been grinding away for five grueling years. I'd been wrong in assuming them some kind of fly-by-night outfit, but I had been correct that he was, in fact, dealing with some anger issues after a bad breakup. I ran out of steam passing through Compiègne, but by Saint-Denis, thirty minutes north of the city, I perked up.

Our hotel reservations were near the venue, La Boule Noire, in the eighteenth arrondissement. The City of Light is celebrated for its eclectic array of architectural styles, from the gothic medieval spires of Notre-Dame to the grand tree-lined boulevards with their Lutetian limestone facades. Because we were driving in from the north, the Sacré-Cœur Basilica, with its distinctive Byzantine domes, should have been visible perched high on the hills of Montmartre, but we found ourselves in a dimly lit burb on a street crowded with squat concrete buildings.

"Your destination is in two hundred yards," Google Maps announced, but that couldn't be right because the hotel seemed less destination, more way station. Everyone was now awake; a pall fell over us as we pulled up to what was a dead ringer for that beacon of mediocrity. Bien sûr que non: an American Econo Lodge. In Paris?

Along with the low price and proximity to the venue, one of the hotel's recommendations was that it offered secure parking, so we brightened seeing an entrance to an underground lot. But as we descended into the belly of the building, the ceiling clearance was at most an inch. We crouched, making that universally recognized compacted "eeeeeeeh" sound. We were your breast in a mammogram.

The lead singer was now seething. "Whoever designed this garage should be drawn and quartered. Whoever designed this garage should be disemboweled. Whoever designed this garage should be castrated." Before he could go full-on French Revolution and suggest guillotining, Jeremy took the wheel, and through careful and deliberate maneuvering deftly managed the hairpin spiral into the catacombs of the building. Along with a take-your-pants-off accent, his steeliness was one of his most attractive qualities. Given my pogrom-fleeing ancestors, hysteria has been epigenetically programmed into my DNA. But any stirrings of desire evaporated when we emerged from the van and were hit with a sulfurous rotten-egg smell—eau de Paris sewer.

Despite our exhaustion, we sprinted up the stairs to the lobby, which had all the Gallic charm of a Rodeway Inn. In the elevator, Jeremy's face was a mask of inscrutability. I averted my eyes, afraid I might sob, but when we opened the door to our room, we were both confused. We were in an undecorated vestibule facing two fire doors. Neither looked promising.

Door number one led to a bathroom that had been painted a tired brown with bronze tile accents and towels in a complementary mood depressor, tired's second cousin: dull beige. It was cave-like, a quality exactly no one wants in a bathroom except maybe a bear.

Door number two led to a bedroom. The heavy metal door clanked shut behind us as we entered and took in the low cottage-cheese ceiling. The flat paint on the scuffed walls was an anemic shade of sallow. The sheets had been laundered so many times they sagged like loose skin. The pillows, defeated; the mattress, moribund. With no give left, there was a thudding sound as I sank down onto the bed.

Hoping for a view, I pushed the floor-to-ceiling curtains aside, but it was a bait and switch. Our cell had a two-by-two-foot window looking out onto what might have been the street, but it was impossible to tell because of the bars affixed to the exterior wall. We were on the fourth floor with no fire escape. We could have been anywhere and nowhere. A Mr. Coffee maker was glued to the top of a sputtering mini fridge. A Mr. Coffee in the city of cafés?

"This is where the terrorists hide out before they plant the bomb," I said. Bending over to take off my shoes, I clocked a smattering of bleach stains on the carpet and a mound of toenail clippings under the bed.

Maybe I'd jumped to conclusions. This was the kind of place where you went to sleep and woke up in an ice-filled bathtub. That would explain the air lock and heavy fire door, better to mask the sound of screaming while your kidney was harvested for sale on the black market. I turned toward Jeremy, who'd been stoically unpacking as he placed a bottle of lube by the bed. "You've got to be kidding. I'm not taking my pants off. I'm not even taking off my socks!" He paused. "Well, at least there are two doors to the bathroom." I had yet to say "I love you" or even consider the possibility, but with that impeccable timing and driest of dry British deliveries, that might be where we were headed.

Jeremy trundled off to brush his teeth, but I didn't. I had no intention of using the bathroom because I was trying to pretend that I was not there, because this could not be where we'd make memories like Bergman and Bogart.

Alone in the room, I had what might be termed a come-to-Jesus moment. Or, since I was on tour with a rock 'n' roll band, a face-the-music moment. I googled the charming hotel my thrifty-minded friend had recommended. Rooms were available. Then I pulled up the website of the dump where we found ourselves and discovered that Jeremy had made an error: Our hotel was part of a chain, and he'd booked the wrong location. Given my potentially abbreviated lifespan, why not stay someplace where toenails of unknown provenance weren't the only amenity that wasn't nailed down? I'd need to upgrade to the other hotel on my own, because it would be bad form for Jeremey to leave the band behind.

I reviewed my goals for the trip. One: Try not to die. As of 2 a.m. I still had a pulse, though I put my chances of surviving the night at fifty-fifty. Two: Romance. No way was that happening tonight. We'd had a good run, and leaving could bring an end to whatever Jeremy and I were doing. Three: I was going to merch my heart out. Thus far, I hadn't earned my keep, though I had added chief navigation officer, electronics charger, drug runner, and band manager's support staff to my unexpected, late-in-life skill set.

During that final push toward Paris, the lead singer had told me how Jeremy had discovered the band at a time when they were drawing crowds you could count on two hands. On one American tour, the budget had been so low Jeremy not only drove the van, he'd shared a room with the drummer. He'd lent the band money, and they'd stayed at his home. He'd been working almost around the clock to keep things running smoothly. I'd assumed that their addressing him as Dad was a nod to his tendency toward dad jokes, which might have been true, but it was also a sign of affection. Jeremy's dedication was endearing. Damn it. I hate when empathy creeps in when you least expect it. I felt a personal growth opportunity coming on. I'd balked whenever I heard the phrase "cancer can be a teacher." Anything cancer had to teach me I would prefer to learn in a different way.

"Please don't feel bad about this place," I'd said when he returned from the bathroom. He looked relieved. "Also, I booked a room at the hotel I'd suggested for when you guys leave for Germany. If I have to spend that extra night here by myself, I'll be found hanging from the ceiling. If someone hasn't stolen an organ from me first. Let's get some sleep. Still no fucking happening!"

Our air-conditioning unit wheezed stale air and emitted a sour mildewy smell, which I would later learn is referred to as "dirty sock scent." This occurs when an evaporator coil is dirty, although it was possible that Jeremy and I were the source of the odor because we had on dirty socks. I strategically folded a scarf over the top of the sheet, creating what I hoped was a sanitizing barrier between my face and the fabric. We held hands, chastely, and mercifully, my super sleep anywhere, anytime power kicked in and I was out.

I woke up an hour earlier than our meetup time with the band, elated to find my organs intact. I slathered on my moisturizer and sunscreen while Jeremy slept. I was down to my one remaining pair of inside-out rotated underwear and my last clean shirt. A hand-dyed raw silk blouse in semolina yellow with cornflower-blue borders. I was going to be the cutest crone at the nightclub.

From the concierge, I learned that we weren't technically in an arrondissement. The hotel was clinging to the Paris city limits by its dirty toenail clippings. But, being Paris adjacent, there was a serviceable café across the street. I downed an espresso, ordered a flaky warm croissant, gnawing only at the crusty end, convinced that if I ingested even a small morsel of nourishment, I'd split a seam. I threw back another espresso, but ça ne fait rien.

Word had spread since the Pinkpop and the show was looking like it might sell out. During the hour it took to crawl through the congested streets of our outer arrondissement and cross the Seine to make our way to Montparnasse, Jeremy muttered his confusion at how it could take so long to get to the venue, but I kept mum about his mistake. The band, still basking in the afterglow of the festival, checked out social media posts from newly minted fans. None of them so much as raised their eyes as we passed by L'Arc de Triomphe.

I wanted to honor Emily's rule to take up as little space as possible, but the band's chattiness was infectious. I chimed in, recalling how amazing it was to see the empty expanse of the festival grounds begin to fill, how the crowd grew to almost ten thousand, how the stage manager had said, "We never do this, it throws the schedule off, but the crowd is demanding it!"

I could be retelling the miracle of Chanukah: "Nes Gadol Haya sham!" as we say in Hebrew when recounting how the Maccabees, an underestimated ragtag bunch of Jewish rebels, defeated a mighty Greek army: A great miracle happened there. Only, that story is rife with supernatural occurrences and based on apocryphal reportage; and I could personally attest to this spectacle.

They nodded along, except the guitarist, who still had not spoken a single word to me. I'd been extra cautious, giving him a wide berth. Since we'd lost time on the magic mushroom run in Rotterdam, he'd fallen behind on his side hustle, editing movie trailers, and was still smarting over his lost suitcase.

A parking spot had been saved for us directly in front of the venue: headliners' privilege. The club was located near the base of Sacré-Coeur, which loomed just above. There were still seven hours until showtime: this would finally be the start of our sightseeing. Jeremy and I had made it only the length of the block when a text arrived. There was good news, bad news, and worst news. The newly minted T-shirts had arrived; our Apple Square, the device for accepting payments, wasn't configured to work in France; and the suitcase was now MIA. It might be in Prague, or it might be in Budapest, or it might have been in some lonesome corner of any number of European airports. The suitcase was (literally) a lost cause, but Jeremy had to find an Apple Store or there'd be no merch sales.

I'd flown across the globe. I'd traveled by van, trolley, and lorry drivers' ferry, survived a drug run, a mosh pit, and a hotel room without a bathroom door to sell merch. I was not going to the Musée d'Orsay. I was going to an Apple Store.

I gazed up at the ghostly white travertine cupolas. The dense pattern adorning the domes looked festive, like the rickrack on the hems of the matching sailor suits my mother had dressed me and my sister in as children. I snapped a selfie, punctuating the beginning, middle, and end of our one day in Paris.

Back at the venue, Square in hand, Jeremy and I were given a rickety folding card table, which we set up in an area that would likely see foot traffic. "Try to sell these old American T-shirts; it will be hard as fans do their research and they want the newest designs," he said. "Also, they're all XXXL." As I affixed T-shirts to a pegboard behind us, I received a lashing rebuke in French—apparently, I was not authorized to wall space. There went my display. I attempted my superior folding technique, but I'd had the band's previous tour logo in mind. I'm an idiot. The new T-shirts, when folded, read EAD POE OCIETY.

I slung the shirts over the sides of the cardboard box, using the four sides, making sure to drape the collar over the inside of the box facing up, so I could spot the sizes more easily. I ordered them clockwise from S, M, L, to XXXL. I was an idiot, but an idiot with a system!

Now that I was on merch duty and an official crew member, I felt entitled to occupy, if not mental, then physical space, and fortify myself with the snacks set aside for band members. Backstage, the green room was a step up from the tent at Pinkpop. There was a large common room with couches and a craft services spread—packaged snack foods—nothing fancy, but miraculously, there were real bathrooms.

I heard the tap, tap, tapping sounds of drumsticks and vocal warm-ups as I rifled through the multigrain bars, bags of chips, and candy bars. Jeremy's words replayed in my head: "The only money the band will see is from the merch sales." Something, maybe the combined weight of the breads of Europe, settled lower, colonizing a territory in my intestinal track. There'd be no snacking for Merch Crone. Snacking might lead to a bathroom break and I couldn't risk it.

I was about to trash a crumbled-up paper bag mixed in with the snack selections, but it was improbably heavy, so I opened it. Inside was a wallet. I checked the ID. It belonged to the guitarist, who was sprawled on an oversized beanbag chair on the balcony level of the green room, engrossed in his computer screen. I tiptoed up the clanky spiral staircase and approached with caution. "Excuse me, Jack. Um, I don't want to *Mom* you, but I found your wallet in this bag of garbage." He fixed me with fierce Giantsbane intensity, but the sound that came out of his mouth was the plaintive whine of a newborn puppy.

"Go ahead and Mom me, Annabelle, Mom me!"

He knew my name! I handed him his wallet. I charged back to my station. I was Band Mom, and I was gonna merch like no one had ever merched!

The doors opened. A gaggle of diehard fans lined up. They included a mother and daughter who'd seen DPS at the festival.

"Wasn't Pinkpop incredible? The crew said they never allow encores on the smaller stages, it was a first!" I trilled, channeling Mama Rose in *Gypsy*.

In my absence, Jeremy had adjusted the table, and my meticulous size ordering had been scrambled. Early birds surged for preshow purchases, and with all the bending, I was working up a sweat. I sold through a short opening act, and then the band took the stage. The house was enveloped in darkness; the stage flooded in light.

No one had mentioned the importance of setting up in a well-lighted area. No one had told me to keep a small lamp or cell phone flashlight handy. No one had said anything about light, probably because everyone would assume that, everyone except me. Fans continued purchasing and I had no idea what sizes I was pulling up, which meant customers were tossing shirts back to me while I processed other orders.

Jeremy stepped behind the table, commandeering the newly purchased Square, a helpful look on his face, but he'd interrupted my flow. "Get out of my way," I barked. "I got this."

I don't *got this* but I was afraid that if I stopped moving, things would only get worse. After I'd sold the last two hoodies with the new design, I got down to the stash of XXXL American-sized tees and blurted out something that would have made my middle school French teacher proud, "Je suis très fatiguée . . . toujours, this T-shirt is perfect for sleeping. Pour . . . dormir!" Cha-ching.

When the show was in full swing, the more senior audience members who'd withdrawn from the center when moshing broke out lingered by my table, but they weren't buying. A matronly woman leaned toward me. "I don't usually like this genre of music, but they're so good," she said.

I pulled out an ace that I'd kept in my back pocket: the sales pitch I felt certain would tug at heartstrings and open wallets. "I'm Dylan, the guitarist's, mother."

"That's so sweet! Do you go on all the tours?"

"Yes, I do!" I said, as I rang up the XXXL T-shirt, not considering how creepy it might be for the band to hear me say that one of their moms comes on all their tours.

"Aw, that's so cute!" gushed two young women, as they purchased super-sized T-shirts pour dormir.

The band played their final song. The crowd was beginning to disperse, but I was on a roll. I pushed CDs and vinyl. When the band emerged to greet the remaining fans, the matron returned to the merch table. "You're Dylan's mother, right? You told me that he's the guitarist, but he was playing bass." This Merch Maven had studied improv. "*Yes, and* he plays guitar too. He's so talented, I couldn't be prouder." And I was proud of him, but not as proud as I was of myself for selling her a T-shirt she'd probably never wear.

I'd sold $1,400 of merch to a crowd of three hundred. It was not their biggest sales number to date, nor was it their smallest. No records had been broken. No headline news made. No one thanked me. I was a good enough Merch Girl.

As we loaded into the van, two dudes attempted to distract Jeremy and the guys and steal their equipment. They were dissuaded without a lot of drama, but now I'd been party to yet another rite of passage on the road. On the way back to the terrorists' hideout, the guys studied their own images on social media and my thoughts turned to Jane Goodall. According to Goodall, when she arrived in Africa to study chimp communities, the chimps scattered when she approached them. One day the male chimps continued their grooming ritual when she sat down among them; she knew that signaled she'd been accepted into the community.

"Come with us to Germany and then on to Copenhagen," Jeremy said on the morning after the gig. It would be such a rock 'n' roll move to say, "Screw it!" but the boulevards were getting wider, the trees leafier, and soon we were turning onto a cobblestone lane that looked like something out of a storybook. The charming hotel my friend had recommended came into view. It had a hand-painted wooden shingle, and in each window there was a flower box overflowing with vines trailing the chalky champagne-colored Lutetian limestone facade.

The band members were on the socials, checking out posts from newer newly minted fans. Jeremy and I embraced quickly. They'd need to beat the midday traffic. He hopped back into the driver's seat, and I dragged my bag across the cobblestone street. It took more energy than anticipated. It was the first time in a week that the misalign-wheeled bag was my responsibility. Jeremy had carried it for me at each of our stops.

I was standing in the hotel's arched stone entryway when the guitarist stepped out of the van. Jack stood in the street, tatted arms outstretched. "It won't be the same without you, Annabelle." I rushed in for the hug and turned away before the first tear landed on my cheek.

My room was even smaller than at the organ-harvesting hostel, but it had a matchbox elegance. The bed was a confection of crisp white linens, puffy pillows, crowned with a cushy down comforter. French doors opened to a view of the neighborhood's chimney tops, the apex of the Eiffel Tower just visible in the distance.

I squinted when I turned on the bathroom lights; it was practically a whiteout. The miniature *chambre* featured sparkling white marble tiles and a row of even whiter towels toasting on a warmer that seemed to have been set to temperature level: *You need this now.* I tore off my clothes, plopped down on the marble shower floor, and let the many shower jets massage my belly.

I felt an urgency akin to giving birth. I ascended the throne and while this effort did not produce another life, I did push something out close to the size of a human baby.

After luxuriating in more hot water than I'd had access to in a week, I swaddled myself in a deep-pile bathrobe, cranked up the air conditioner, threw open the French doors, and bathed in the cross stream of warm air and the cool ozone-depleting artificial current. Yes, I was a wasteful American, and I was okay with it!

I snapped a selfie in the bathrobe and sent it to Jeremy. We're spending the night in dormitory bunk beds on a communal farm in Germany! he texted back. How wonderful for them, I thought, grateful that "them" didn't include me.

At the corner bistro, I ordered steak frites and devoured every morsel as well as a couple of stray frites that had migrated over from the table next to mine. I stopped into a bakery and purchased a cinnamon brioche. The brioche had the feathery consistency of cotton candy. It was dusted with a sugary film so light it might have been blown from the breath of fairies. I wolfed it down right there in the street like an animal. I'd like to say that my motivation was Proustian, that I'd ordered and inhaled another in hopes that this bun might serve as my madeleine one day, but the truth was, I just couldn't help myself.

Jeremy and I would never have Paris, but according to the hotel's old-timey map, the Musée d'Orsay was about twenty minutes away. From there, I'd walk to Café de Flore and be a few steps from the Pont des Arts. The bridge is what draws Carrie Bradshaw to Paris in the season one finale of the *Sex and the City* reboot *And Just like That* . . .

Carrie was desperate for closure after a year spent mourning the death of her husband, John, aka Mr. Big. We find her on the Pont des Arts, which happens to be the very spot where she and Big rekindled their love affair. Moonlit, swathed in oodles of organza, milking the maudlinness of the moment, she unlatches the catch on her Timmy Woods Eiffel Tower $4,800 (I looked it up) handbag and unburdens herself of John's ashes. It seemed a tad selfish on Carrie's part, as John's family had wished him to rest in the family mausoleum; nevertheless, she scatters his remains with swanning, operatic import. Dumping ashes in the Seine happens to be illegal, but whatevs: She's Big's widow and can afford the fine.

To move forward, she must leave something behind and do so in the most fabulous outfit, in the most fabulously over-the-top gesture, in the most fabulous location. And just like that, she's ready to move on.

Me? I'd showered but was back in my Merch Girl uniform. Last night's sweat had rendered my blouse a shade darker, "UTI-suspected urine sample" yellow. I had on grimy jeans, mud-caked loafers, and was carrying a tote made from a recycled tarp. If only I could, with one distinct gesture, achieve closure to this chapter of my life. Maybe the blood supply to my brain had been diverted to my digestive system, but I felt something shifting as cinnamon sugar dribbled down the front of my dirty shirt. I'd fretted about finding myself in a *no light at the end of the tunnel* existence. But I'd made that clean well-lighted tunnel my home. And just like that, on my last day on the continent, on what might be my last day in Paris, ever, I chucked my list of "things to do in Paris before you die," as if I would always be granted more days, more time, more Paris.

I wandered. Strolling down one street and then another, channeling Chet Baker, who'd recorded "Let's Get Lost" in Paris. What did I see? A certain slant of light, cherry blossoms swirling like confetti. Nothing remarkable, the same everyday phenomena that had brought me to my knees a year ago. Only now my emotions weren't so close to the surface.

I walked an hour or three. I found myself in a passageway—a tiny artery stemming from a boulevard. I'd meant to get lost in a metaphorical allusion to Chet Baker but not actually get lost. Maybe it was because I was the only person walking around with a paper map in my hand, or it was that, having pooped, I was positively radiant, but a kind Parisian pointed me in the right direction.

Rounding a corner, I spotted the shingle of my hotel. I stopped for a glass of wine at the corner bistro. "When you're on tour, the whole world stops," the lead singer had said to me in Surrey. I'd forgotten that. For one week, I hadn't been Annabelle Gurwitch, a person living with stage 4 cancer, an identity that had defined almost every waking moment over the past two years. Band Mom was not Cancer Mom. I'd never said, "While we're on tour, don't talk to me about cancer." The band never asked a single question about me because they were all twenty-seven, in Europe for the first time, on a tour they hoped would change their lives. I'd sold $1,400 of their merch and they'd given me the gift of indifference.

Seizing the day like it's your last? Better to pluck the day. To live each day as if it were your first, with curiosity and wonder, as if you know nothing and expect nothing. I'd indulged in an obscene extravagance. I'd frittered away the hours. I'd had an ordinary day, the most rare and precious state for someone facing their mortality. I'd left the end of my life behind on tour, not with an extravagant gesture, but through intention, unobservable to those around me.

Also, I hadn't done anything illegal, except that it might be considered actionable to be in Paris and not visit a single attraction.

Henry Miller wrote that "one's destination is never a place but rather a new way of looking at things."

The server at the bistro delivered l'addition and ordered me to vacate my table. But he wasn't practicing that patented Parisian service industry impudence; all the tables and chairs were being removed. It was June 21, the summer solstice, the longest day of the year. Each year since 1982, Paris has celebrated Fête de la Musique. DJs spin until dawn and the streets fill with free live performances, some staged and others springing up spontaneously. I might have had an ordinary day, but nobody puts Paris in a corner.

The sun was setting, and people were convening at the end of the block, where a DJ was spinning house music, and a crowd spilled out onto the sidewalk. I waded through one crowd, then another, and another, up and down the neighboring streets. The air vibrated with music and laughter. I might have caught a contact high as waves of weed smoke wafted my way.

Resistance was futile. I followed the sound of drumming to a café where North African musicians were jamming. The beat thrummed through my body.

Revelers surged onto the street. In a few hours, I would be home and resume my dialogue with impermanence, but on this longest day, impermanence was my well-lighted tunnel. I had tasted the close to fine wine and the cheap beer. I was not stuck in the traffic in Paris; I was the traffic in Paris.

The midsummer moon hung low and luminous. The café lights blazed bright. A warm breeze blew, sticky with sweat and champagne. The earth was tilting toward the sun, and I was dancing on the eleventh-century cobblestone streets of Paris.

Like Cherished Friends We Rarely Get a Chance to See

During those first few months of treatment, I was leaning heavily on Alexander Pushkin. Not the writer, but my cat, who, for reasons lost to time, shared a name with the Russian poet. He and his brother had entered my life seven years earlier; the two gingers had been abandoned in an alley behind a hair salon. I went in for a cut and color and walked out with cats. Ezra, in grade school at that time, announced that one of them would be named Perkins—who can recall why? Maybe we had a book about Hollywood and Anthony Perkins was on the cover? I didn't try to talk him out of it. In the naming of things, children are tuned in to the music of the spheres, and you really shouldn't fuck with that. I can't remember if there was a reason other than trying to come up with the least likely historical figure to be paired with Anthony Perkins when the name Pushkin popped into my head. Of the Russians, I'd preferred Tolstoy's tragic women to Pushkin's self-absorbed men, but the names stuck.

Ezra and I bottle-fed the kittens, and they matured into expert snugglers and excellent mousers. Initially, I tried and failed to make Perkins and Pushkin indoor cats. They'd mew at the front door, insisting on liberation, intent on roaming, but sauntered home without fail every evening for cuddles and canned food. They tag-team hunted, turning the living room into a killing field. It wasn't unusual to find a disembodied rodent head, face frozen in a death mask, every bit the vermin version of Edvard Munch's *The Scream*. One cat would sport a Cheshire grin; the other had a hint of tail sticking out of the corner of his mouth, like a cowboy sucking straw.

Perkins provided steadfast cat companionship, but Pushkin had that thing they call "it" with actors. A John Travolta *Saturday Night Fever* swagger. He bestrode the neighborhood's narrow streets like a colossus. He sidled up to neighbors and the odd passersby. Friends visiting from out of town, cat-sitters, and neighbors were fond of photographing Pushkin, aka "the mayor" of our block.

Perkins disappeared one night in 2018. I'll never know what fate befell him. Most likely, an appetizer for local coyotes. Perkins's absence reverberated through our household like a tear in the fabric holding our family together. Then, as my *after life* commenced, the daily routine of caring for my remaining cat gave shape to my days as time seemed to be folding in on itself. When Ezra moved into an apartment, I'd started cradling Pushkin like a baby, patting his back as though burping him. *This is how it starts. Soon I'll be wearing him out in public in a sling*, I thought, and I was okay with that.

So when Pushkin suddenly stopped eating, appeared bloated and glassy-eyed, I couldn't bear the thought of losing the comforting skin-to-fur contact. For a month, I threw money I didn't have at a dazzling array of tests, scans, and an exploratory surgery. Was it rat poisoning, a bowel obstruction, a tumor? Between the Covid-protocol-mandated curbside drop-offs and rushed phone calls with the vet, there was some strange symmetry to the fact that both my cat and I were going it alone to medical appointments.

After $5,000 and with no definitive answers, I faced a choice: authorize a costly exploratory surgery with no guarantees except a difficult recovery or put an end to Pushkin's suffering. "I've just started treatment for cancer. I can't handle making decisions. What should I do?" I asked the vet, ugly-crying in the office's parking lot. I hoped he would offer words of comfort. I hoped he'd assure me that he understood my worry over incurring more costs and inflicting pointless suffering. I hoped he'd make the decision for me. He offered nothing.

I was still inconsolable when Pushkin's ashes arrived in the mail, three weeks later.

His mourners included an employee from a home security company whose route took him past my home regularly. A week after Pushkin's death, I was weeding the front garden when he pulled over and asked after Pushkin; he'd grown so attached that he'd begun bringing cans of food and feeding Pushkin, who returned the favor by keeping him company while he ate lunch in his patrol car. How many meals had that cat been scarfing down each day?

"How can I ever fill the hole he's left in my life?" I asked every friend who would listen.

"You need kittens, STAT," said my friend Bart, a theater director I'd worked with numerous times and who'd become a close friend. Bart was also a cat lover who swore that his cat winked, conspiratorially, on occasion. In the past, it had seemed appropriate to observe a waiting period, a few months between the loss of a family pet and the introduction of a new one. I didn't have the luxury of time. Bart was right.

I needed comfort. I needed something to care for. I needed an excuse to buy that fishing pole wand with a felt bird, colorful feathers, and ribbons.

Only, in pandemic-era Los Angeles, there was a dog-eat-dog competition for kittens. Californians hoping to add a dog to their household were driving to Wisconsin for a terrier. I contacted every cat rescue within fifty miles. Each had a name more cleverly contrived than the last: the Cat's Meow, the Catty Wagon, and the Kitty Bungalow Charm School for Wayward Cats.

In short order, my phone was flooded with photos of big-eyed tabbies, fluffy Siberians, and prissy-faced Ragdolls.

Grammy, Emmy, Oscar, Razzy, Epsy, Olive, Inky, Fang, Stripes, and Raisin. These are just a few of the kittens I tried to adopt. At a year old, Raisin was technically a cat, not a kitten, but I'd hoped to welcome her into my home as a pity rescue, because what kind of person names a cat Raisin?

The waiting lists were lengthy and the application process was more rigorous than applying for citizenship. Rescuers demanded virtual home walk-throughs, proof of past cat stewardship, knowledge of local laws and ordinances governing pet ownership, reference letters. Were we rehoming royalty?

"Would a recommendation from another cat suffice?" I asked in one email.

A month into my search, I was granted an audience with two feral Maine coons by a rough-and-tumble rescuer who assured me that, with patience, they'd go from "hissy to homey." It sounded promising, if terrifying. I drove two hours south of L.A. for an outdoor meetup and potential handoff.

"Wear gloves, for protection," she'd said.

"You mean for Covid safety?" I asked.

"No. For your safety."

I arrived at the appointed location, an apartment building in an unfamiliar neighborhood, and was issued new instructions. She'd left the apartment unlocked. I was to enter, head straight down a hallway and into a den where I'd have the opportunity to meet the cats, which for safety purposes—mine—had been placed inside a playpen.

You're definitely out of your comfort zone, I congratulated myself. Along with being masked, I'd donned oven mitts for extra protection. I felt every bit like I had been dropped into an *SNL* sketch, portraying a Navy Seal on deployment to apprehend a feline criminal cartel.

I entered the dimly lit apartment. Only then did it dawn on me that this might be some kind of shakedown targeting cat ladies. Who was an easier mark for scamming? Just flash us a photo of a round-eyed fur baby and we're reeled in. "Please, pay them what they want," I'd plead in the video they'd send to my family. "What could I do? They sent a photo of a long-haired Himalayan. Do you know how rare they are?"

Sure enough, in an empty den, there was a tented kid's Pack 'n Play containing two seething creatures thrashing about. It was kitty Cujo. "Former TV Hostess Turned Spinster Felled by Feral Felines!" the *New York Post* story would read. "And we thought the cancer would get her," my sister would be quoted as saying. I hightailed it out of there.

"Sometimes saying no can be saying yes to yourself," Bart said.

Determined to move to the front of the cuddly clowder lines, I upped my cat lady cred, sending cat selfies along with each application. "What's that on my head? It's a cat!" "Yes, that's a cat lounging on my keyboard . . . burrowing in my laundry basket . . . snuggling under my bed covers."

The pictures did the trick. I was now in the running to adopt Pablito (a tuxy) and Nutmeg (a calico).

Pablito and Nutmeg's foster mom required those of us vying for them to FaceTime with her and the kittens as a sort of chemistry test. I cooed convincingly enough to make it to the next level in the competition. To proceed, she said, I would be required to sign a contract pledging to grant the kitties "free reign over my household" and vow that "cats are family." I'd be bound to instruct my new "family members" in "Proper Cat Behavior." Exactly whose criteria of PCB wasn't specified. If T. S. Eliot's, that might mean dancing by the light of the Jellicle moon. If Big or Little Edie, the kittens could be permitted to view every surface in my house as their litter box. (I'd seen *Grey Gardens* several times.) Signing the contract also entitled the rescuer to "unlimited visitation rights," which should have been the deal-breaker, but the part of the contract that troubled me most was to agree that "cats are family" and to treat them as such.

I'd always bristled at the suggestion that pets were family members. I understood the impulse, but was "family" really the correct label? A friend had recently begun calling her Pomeranian, Lucy, "her dogter." That seemed worrisome. And cats are, let's be honest, "trusted associates" at best. There's a tendency to want to assume more of them than evidence suggests we should. Stories of lost cats traveling great distances to make it home get circulated from time to time, but do these cats love their people or do they love their places? I was once granted visitation rights with a cat that I'd shared years of my life with, whose custody I lost in a breakup. My heart was brimming with affectionate memories, but the cat, ensconced in her new home, looked through me with the dull blankness of a server on the graveyard shift after you say you'll just be ordering coffee, and would it be all right if you sat there awhile.

A 2021 study of auditory capabilities confirmed that cats can distinguish their owners' voices and even register their names. They understand you; they just don't always want to come when called.

Readers were outraged, testifying to their cats' unfettered devotion. I don't find the limits of feline affection in any way disappointing. On the contrary, I find it exciting to share my home with mysterious creatures with whom any expression of affection is an unexpected win.

Beloved pet, yes; family member, no. Fur baby, no; member of household, yes.

I knew that the cat rescuer meant that she wanted me to agree that I would be a responsible and attentive caretaker. But I take words seriously, and how many of us regularly exclaim that our families are driving us crazy? The characterization of family as the epitome of affection was suspect. A large percentage of murders are committed by family members.

Shouldn't the measure of a deep, abiding connection with a sentient being, chipped or otherwise, be that you treat them with the solicitousness reserved for cherished friends you rarely get a chance to see?

"You know this is a nonbinding contract," Bart said.

I did. Still.

With my mortality in question, this might be the last contract I entered into. It seemed important not to misrepresent a long-held, if derived from a possibly flawed and certainly of no monumental importance, conviction. To sign or not to sign seemed like a litmus test of my ethical compass. If not now, when would be the right time to embrace moral rectitude?

Like most of us, I suspect, I'd lived by a slippery code of ethics. Failures included being an inveterate cheater at childhood board games. Anxiety over losing had compelled me to embezzle Monopoly money; I'd cheated in the Game of Life; attempted card counting in Go Fish but was thwarted by being terrible at math. And maybe I'd fed my addiction to expensive hotel bath soaps and body lotions through repeated calls to housekeeping, or even unscrewed the large, environmentally friendly wall-mounted shower containers to siphon the contents into reusable water bottles, but they budget for that too, right? Call me guilty for not coming to a complete stop when making right turns—otherwise known as a "California rolling stop."

Pablito's scrawny black-and-white body and Nutmeg's scrumptious ginger gangliness called to me. Picking the wrong battles to wage was another core value that might be worth leaving behind. I have remained resolutely emoji-free since they entered mainstream usage. I took a stand against the reductiveness of the emoticon and its kinsmen: thumbs up and down, eggplants, and prayer hands. It's pointless and a time suck, but I am still typing out "Heart Emoji" and "Face Blowing Kiss" in text, and I couldn't bring myself to sign that stupid contract.

This is why it's important to make people feel guilty, especially when undeserved. Emily—the musician-dating writer who'd recommended the urgent care that led to my diagnosis—came through.

"I gave you cancer," she said. "Now, I'm giving you cats."

Someone on her mom LISTSERV had unexpectedly come into kittens. Two remained from the litter: Shirley and Betty.

Inviting these cats into my home presented yet another conundrum. Shirley and Betty were kitschy names, which might have seemed like a hoot when I was twenty. It's like furniture: when you're young, it's eccentric and cool to fill your home with antiques. But once you reach a certain age, your antiques make you look like Grandma Moses. If I told anyone I had a Shirley and a Betty living with me, they would think I *was Golden Girl*ing with my mahjongg group. More important, my mother, Shirley, passed in 2016, and it seemed sacrilegious to be calling out, "Shirley, come and get your kibble."

"Darling, you do know that you can change their names?" Bart said. I did.

The kittens' household was off the same freeway as that fateful urgent care. California 2 will always be my portal to cancer and cats. The family greeted me in the driveway. The parents looked to be in their late thirties; the kids, four and six, lurked shyly as I entered the garage, where a cozy nook outfitted with blankets and stuffed animals, a kitten crèche, had been lovingly constructed. A solemnity hung in the air as I was introduced to Simone, the kitten's mother. The cats had been named by the children and, hence, inviolate, so I didn't question the logic that had resulted in Simone's kittens receiving the names Betty and Shirley.

Simone, her body taut with attentiveness, craned her long cat neck, following my every move as I scooped the two into a carrying case. She glued herself to my side as we slow-walked down the driveway to my car and I loaded them into the passenger seat. "I'll take care of Betty and Shirley for you, Simone," I repeated. Simone stood watch, ears at attention, with the family, like a military send-off. No way I could change their names now.

It's been four years since "the ladies," as Bart dubbed them, came to live with me. Shirley and Betty enjoy trying to escape the confines of the house, but I've held firm this time. Shirley is body positive and on the husky side, while Betty is rocking a retro Kate Moss, heroin-chic vibe. They've calibrated their meows to achieve the perfect guilt-inducing pitch when vying for attention.

Shirley sits beside the tub when I take a bath, like a bathroom attendant, waiting patiently for her gratuity—the privilege of slurping from the tub faucet. Betty is a squealer. She prances around the house like a pony, sliding toys under the bedroom door with the hope of more playtime, especially very late into the night.

And what of the reckoning, an impending deathbed conversion to adoption of a strict code of ethics? Evaluating your actions with your final act in mind is a useful exercise, but this is the problem of outliving your expected expiration date: It's a high bar to maintain. I've smuggled THC gummies across international borders, and I might have deducted a meal I treated my son to as a business expense on my taxes, although we did discuss inclusion of him in this book, so technically that might be justified. But all's well that ends well, at least concerning kittens. I'm sure Nutmeg and Pablito found good homes and I have kept my pledge to Simone.

Each morning, after I've downed my numerous espressos, I greet Shirley and Betty with identic enthusiasm, as if we hadn't performed this same ritual the day before, and the day before that. "Good morning, girls! It's so good to see you! Let's get you some breakfast! I'm the luckiest person in the world to get to wake up to your beautiful faces," I say with more ardor than I have ever mustered for family members, but just like I reserve for cherished friends I rarely get a chance to see.

What Would Judy Do?

Fish are not supposed to float upside down.

I was seated in a lonely waiting room in a hospital basement. CT scans are often conducted in basements because the machines weigh close to a thousand pounds. We'd passed no one as an attendant ushered me to this *Land of the Lost*. I was the only "customer," as he put it, that day. None of the 4,000 works of art that grace the walls and grounds of this facility had made it to this remote bay. The sole reading material was *Departures* magazine. Whose brilliant idea was that? But there was an aquarium.

Watching fish swim has been shown to calm the nervous system. Except the aquarium appeared to be empty.

Then I saw it. A single purplish, sardine-like finger-length creature, its color identical to the coral display. Honestly, it was a bit annoying to have to squint to locate the fish that is supposed to keep my blood pressure in check. Then I noticed her body, bent at a funny angle, kinked. The eye, I could see only one, was cloudy.

I tapped on the glass. "Little fish, little fish. Wake up, little fish." Its gills flapped erratically as it struggled to breathe. "Are you okay, little fish?" I asked, panic tightening the muscles of my chest and neck. I signed on to the hospital website and looked up ectothermic animal health, aquarium maintenance, and then janitorial services, but I couldn't find any listing. I dialed the operator.

"There's a fish in distress. Can you send someone to the basement, ASAP? No, it's not a person. It's a fish. A fish in an aquarium isn't breathing."

This didn't make sense to the operator.

"Isn't there someone in charge of aquatic health?" She connected me to housekeeping, but fish weren't their purview. Hyperventilating, I fired off an email.

> Hi, I'm getting a CT scan this morning at the imaging center and in the waiting room downstairs there is a fish in the aquarium that seems to be on her last legs, or maybe that's not an appropriate phrase here. I wanted to alert the maintenance staff because watching a fish struggle to breathe might not be the most comforting entertainment for patients waiting for scans! Hope the little fish will be okay.

In the under forty-five minutes that it took to complete the scan, cross the sky bridge from the medical offices to cancer HQ, and ride the elevator to my appointment with my oncologist, I had earned a reputation as the crazy fish lady.

"I heard you had a problem with a fish?" was the greeting I received at the oncology nurses' station.

Call me nuts, but when a visit costs more than twenty thousand dollars, I think you should be treated to a hot stone massage, a lap dance, and aquariums with live fucking fish!

Judy would never make a scene like that. When Judy got cancer, she never complained. Judy was a model patient. Judy was a cheerful soldier during chemo, whose thousand-watt smile lit up the chemo ward. Judy was also a fictional character in a television series.

When the cancer storyline appears in a series, it's typically several seasons into a successful run. We are primed to the "cancer experience" through numerous, by now well-known telltale visual cues. Characters lose their hair while undergoing chemo, thin to skeletal, and their skin takes on a waxen hue. They valiantly brave their attendant struggles; they either get cured or sadly succumb. Cue the waterworks.

In season three of the wonderfully irreverent *Dead to Me*, Judy, played by Linda Cardellini, receives a stage 4 cervical cancer diagnosis. Spoiler alerts ahead.

I was drawn to *Dead to Me* for its dark comic escapism about an unlikely friendship. The cancer storyline was a twist I hadn't seen coming. I couldn't help but view Judy and myself as mirror world reflections, even if at times it seemed a fun house mirror (fishy) distortion.

I cheered when Jen, Judy's BFF (played by Christina Applegate), ponied up for a "cooling cap" to preserve Judy's hair during chemo. Hair loss is preferable to loss of life, and kudos to everyone who embraces the bald, but I related to Judy's desire to remain recognizable. Targeted therapies like mine rarely cause hair loss, but appearances are entwined with identity and that's not something we can pretend away.

"Would it be possible to get a facelift while I'm in treatment?" I asked my oncologist during one of our first appointments. "Is it okay to be vain when you have cancer?" I whispered, embarrassed by saying the quiet part out loud.

"It wouldn't be a problem," he said, shrugging. "I'm vain too."

That was one of the only times I've been happy with a doctor dismissing my concern. He confided that he was also going through treatment for cancer (a different kind) but wanted to look good for his wife. The question remains a hilarious hypothetical. I'd asked that before realizing how destabilizing dealing with a chronic disease would be to my financial health.

Judy graciously accepts support. When Jen invites her to move in with her family, she's the ideal houseguest, spending quality time with Jen's children, baking cookies, careful to shield them from any uncomfortable, disease-related emotional mood swings. She's as adorkable as ever!

Not me. I had collapsed emotionally in front of my kid, picked fights with my besties, and was only a functional human because of my sister's spreadsheets and graciousness in forgiving my turkey-zucchini-loaf ingratitude.

Judy spreads sunshine wherever she goes, endearing herself to the hospital staff, and she's productive. She uses the time during chemo infusions to fold origami cranes, and when she comes home, she's a wee bit tired, so she takes naps, falling asleep with a beatific smile on her face.

Amen, sister. Napping had become an essential part of my everyday life, although I can be a drooler. I also tried to emulate Judy's sunny disposition, expressing appreciation for every person I interacted with during my visits. On TV, Judy buddied up with the same doting nurse assigned to her care at a cozy chemo center, while each of my appointments entailed numerous procedures which meant zigzagging across the campus and interacting with dozens of nurses, technicians, and staffers; all caring, but aside from the oncologist's immediate staff, I rarely encountered the same folks twice. Somewhere around episode six of season three, while Judy sailed along, I developed a paralyzing fear of needles.

A phlebotomist was attempting to place an IV line and the third time wasn't the charm. Stabbing pain accompanied each jab as if my vein was being Roto-Rootered with a fire iron. Warmth flooded my chest, like a menopausal hot flash. My blood pressure dropped. I slid from the chair to the floor, nauseated and dizzy, on the edge of losing consciousness and control of bodily functions. A gurney was brought in and a cold pack applied to my neck.

"I'm so sorry, I'm swo swowwy . . ." I mumbled to the technician and another patient waiting for their IV line, hoping the latter wasn't a first-timer whom I'd freaked out.

This is what's called a vasovagal reflex. A sudden drop in blood pressure and heart rate. "Do you want to go home and try again tomorrow?" they asked.

I'd driven over an hour in traffic. I'd fasted, had a blood draw, and swilled a sickeningly sweet iodinated solution. If I slunk home now, it would be even harder to return. From the gurney, I called my sister, who knew it was scan day.

"Quick! I need cuteness."

Without missing a beat, she launched into a story about her grandkids. With her distraction and the assistance of a more experienced phlebotomist, we pressed on.

But my sister wouldn't always be available. There were many more needles in my future. I asked myself, what would Judy do?

Judy was the embodiment of keep calm and carry on.

Over the next months, I experimented, like Goldilocks. I tried chattiness but launching into one of my free-ranging monologues tired me out. THC gummies helped me relax but I was even more chatty when stoned, which tired others out. I tried singing, but I'd already earned the reputation as crazy fish lady; now I was going to be eccentric singing lady? The "just right" turned out to be a kind of active listening, summoning the genuine curiosity I have when

I interview other authors. One of the joys of a writing career is serving as interlocuter at author events.

"Would you mind if I asked you a few questions while we do this? It helps me relax. What music are you listening to?" I'd ask each phlebotomist.

Music was the topic that yielded the most lively and engaging exchange, and since discovering I could love heavy metal music, or at least one band in that genre, I'd become fascinated with musical preferences. I'm also such a people pleaser that I wouldn't dream of mentioning my discomfort while a nurse describes how fado changed her life. It took a few visits before I worked my way from the gurney to a La-Z-Boy recliner and then back to the hard-backed cushion-free contraption that looks too much like an adult high chair but which I knew was more convenient for the busy staff. Maybe the scenes where Judy's bubbliness lost its fizz were cut for time.

One story point in *Dead to Me* hit a little too close to the bone.

"You know—you can't untell people," Naomi, a producer I was working with, advised when I was debating about publishing my diagnosis. "No one will ever treat you the same way."

Judy knows this as well. When her cancer comes back after a period of remission, she waits months before she tells Jen and her family. She doesn't want anyone to make a fuss. Not to worry. Jen insists Judy move from the pool house into the main house.

But Judy doesn't lose sleep worrying over the impact of her treatment to her employment or the hit to her identity. Due to circumstances related to her being a fictional character, Judy doesn't have to work. She's stolen money from the Greek Mafia, which makes her both a criminal and complicit in criminal activity. She's a little murder-y too, which is also troubling, but she uses her ill-gotten gain to pay off Jen's debt, buy Jen's kid a car, and cover her own treatment. So, you go, girl; your felonies can be forgiven. Though she'd been a devoted and, of course, sainted art instructor at a senior home, her sense of self-worth wasn't wrapped up in that job.

Real life is a bit more complicated.

"I'm not afraid of cancer anymore," my friend Jill had said during one of our Sunday Stammtisches.

"Really?" I asked, hoping she'd share her secret sauce.

"A teacher I work with, Beth, has cancer, and she's doing amazingly. Beth's unstoppable," she said.

I called Beth. Beth is an extraordinarily resilient person with a genuine passion for teaching. She also needs a cane to walk, help to rise from the toilet, and has difficulty reading. Since our conversation, she has taken early retirement.

It hadn't occurred to Jill that Beth hadn't confided in her out of fear she might be perceived as someone who couldn't pull her weight, which might lead to her firing, or reassignment to a lesser compensated and less advantageous position.

Fear of losing her job was what motivated one of my mentees to keep her stage 4 diagnosis a secret from her employers. She worked a demanding job whose income her family was dependent on and she suspected this news wouldn't be well received. (Some forms of employment have federal protections, however, there are loopholes, and many people in treatment are unceremoniously kicked to the curb.) She's also kept the news from all but her family members. She sometimes had severe reactions to the medication, the rash turning to open sores on her head, which were mitigated by injecting fluids. She says it made her look like the Elephant Man. On those days, she worked from home. She even missed a girlfriend getaway beach weekend because of it. I can't imagine forgoing any chance to swim in the ocean or receive love from friends. She's also never gotten to be the recipient of a juicer. She steadfastly pursued this strategy, and it's not my role to change her mind. On the plus side, she'd been able to remain entirely herself, and there's benefit in that.

She has also never received this kind of text.

You smoked to be thin.

I burst into tears. The text was from a number that wasn't in my contacts. Why had someone written this to me? Who hated me this much? Did I have enemies? What did it mean, anyway? I'd bummed cigarettes on film sets in my twenties, but was it to avoid snacking? I could imagine having said that because no one liked hearing you were naturally thin, but I couldn't remember doing so. Was this person challenging my veracity? Was this a possible extortion scheme? What kind of monster seeks to assign blame to someone with cancer?

When you have bone or pancreatic cancer, no one interrogates your behavior or sits in judgment over whether you deserve sympathy, but that's what occurs with lung cancer. Despite this being a misinformed notion—exposure to environmental toxins, in the form of either air pollution or radon gas, is the number two cause of lung cancer, and most likely why I'd developed the disease—it's a dangerous calculus. Once we go down the road of perceived personal responsibility, it's a slippery slope. Do we deny care to people who tanned in their teenage years and develop skin cancer later? Do we count the number of Happy Meals consumed to determine the resources we devote to a diabetic? A pack-a-day habit gets no sympathy, but a pack-a-year habit is forgivable?

Judy, with cervical cancer, has no such problems.

Judy didn't need a cancer support group either, though ironically, Judy and Jen's friendship began at a grief support group when mourning the loss of loved ones in season one. As I became more acclimated to life in Cancerland, leaning more heavily on its residents became essential. I forged closer ties with my fellows. At some point each day, I'd scroll through the Facebook group to quell the gnawing hollow that can take me by surprise. Our members announce happy milestones: *It's my seven-year cancerversary, never give up hope!* Loved ones give us news of passings. When Dann Wonser's death was announced the entire community mourned him. He'd gotten eighteen years after a stage 4 diagnosis and countless lines of treatment. Dann kept a diary online and though we'd never spoken, we'd corresponded in emails. I'd thanked him for being such a beacon of hope.

Sometimes, I'll lurk, but I had to jump into the conversation when I saw this post: *I know you all are warriors, so I'm chagrined to admit this, but I'm going in for a needle biopsy today and I'm scared. I'm just a big baby.*

It's okay, I wrote, *I'm a big baby too!* A cascade of *I'm a Big Baby* posts followed. I was awfully proud of us for allowing space for such vulnerability and I can't imagine my life now without this outlet.

I'm not trying to pull rank here, but Judy's ability to keep calm and carry on might have been tested if Judy had more than one kind of cancer.

"Annabelle, I'm so sorry to tell you this, but a radiologist noticed a suspicious mass in your right breast on your lung CT scan." Razmig, my oncologist's nurse practitioner, was so sympathetic during this phone call that I apologized on my boob's behalf for causing him to have to make that call. Another "incidentaloma," an incidental finding, as it's called. Cue more scans, and biopsies of numerous suspicious areas, and a resulting diagnosis: DCIS, a ductal carcinoma in situ. So much for being a cancer slacker. Talk about overachieving, a second cancer? A DCIS is actually a stage 0 precursor to breast cancer, and entirely unrelated to lung cancer and the targeted therapy, which was good news, because lung cancer can spread to the breast. And it had to be dealt with.

I took a workmanlike approach, which, let's face it, Judy surely would have done. When diagnosed with an early-stage cancer while in treatment for a late-stage one, it puts the lesser one in perspective. I sprang into action, without stopping for a second opinion. Sarah accompanied me to the hospital for a lumpectomy and Jeremy escorted me home later that day. My surgeon determined that I wouldn't need radiation, and also, we'd want to protect that area for possible future lung radiation.

I'd managed to fulfill the oncologist's hope that I would live long enough to get breast cancer. This was actually great news, possible only because of the biomarker therapies, but I'd need to be monitored more closely for breast cancer.

Two weeks post-surgery, I flew to Chicago to attend the American Society of Clinical Oncology (ASCO) Conference. The annual event draws forty thousand oncology professionals from across disciplines. I'd been invited to attend as a patient advocate member and was determined not to miss it, bandages and all.

One of the highlights of a two-cancer experience is that I've experienced the onboarding process for both. At my first breast cancer appointment, I received a binder containing a cornucopia of useful information: tips on nutrition, discount coupons for gyms, counseling resources, and a list of support groups, including Imerman Angels. Also: a free recovery bra!

By that point, I'd been through lung cancer onboarding with two hospital systems. I'd received no binder with the information I'd craved for months that could have interrupted my punishing isolation. This is an example of how greater funding can impact patients' lives in tangible ways. The binders were prepared by the Susan G. Komen Breast Cancer Foundation, while lung cancer advocacy and research remain underfunded; despite accounting for 25 percent of cancer deaths in the U.S., it has historically received 9 percent of federal cancer research. We don't actually have an accurate current statistic because the Department of Defense lung cancer research funding, which represents a significant percentage, was zeroed out in 2025. Lung cancer is, to use a *Brady Bunch* metric, the Jan of cancers, the neglected middle child. It's all *Marcia, Marcia, Marcia*. Breast, breast, breast.

The only thing not included in the binder was a hug, but the breast surgeon gave me one; she's a hugger and I appreciated it.

The first time Judy goes into remission, she gets to "ring the bell," that ritual marking of the conclusion of chemo. On my way into the hospital, I'll see staff lined up as a patient passes through, like the *Soul Train* showcase. They clap as the patient exits, heading back to a world where they could be hit by a bus, but they've checked cancer off their list of possible causes of death for that day. Those of us doing *the best we can for as long as we can* are not afforded such celebrations, although our doctors might tell us to break out the champagne.

Will cancertainments tackle life in the age of precision medicine? Without those tropes and visual cues, it might not feel cinematic. But there is nuance.

Sydney, who's an active member of our advocacy community, was diagnosed while in medical school, toughed it out, and practices as an emergency room physician in Maryland. She had to harvest her eggs prior to going on the TKI, a biomarker targeted therapy; it's teratogenic, and it will add stress and cost when she and her husband decide to have children. I'd watch that show.

Alas, Judy's cancer inevitably returns and she dies. But before that, she carries out well-executed plans. She folds a thousand origami cranes for Jen's kid, reconnects with her estranged mother, sets a series of events in motion that will ensure Jen's well-being, and she and Jen enjoy a vacay at a beach house in Mexico.

Judy, ever the considerate companion, steals away silently, slipping into the ocean while Jen sleeps off tequila shots. We don't see Judy's end, but we are left to imagine that it was swift and painless.

Judy had worked in a senior home as a caregiver, and she was so unfailingly selfless that she probably stopped to help a struggling fish on her way out to sea. It would be *so* Judy to have fish-resuscitation skills at her fingertips.

As much as returning to water holds an appeal, I wouldn't want to ruin the ocean for my son. But I have tried to think proactively, like Judy. On a recent visit to New York, Jessica and Neena and I met for breakfast. They've gotten used to having me around for longer, so we're able to speak about my health without ressurecting the great goodbye ritual.

"Listen," I said, between bites of a walnut-and-raisin scone, "I just read *In Love*, Amy Bloom's account of how she and her husband dealt with early-onset dementia."

"I read that," Jessica said, not looking up from her yogurt and granola.

"So, as you know, she accompanies him to Dignitas, the place in Switzerland where you can exit life on your own terms, and—"

Jessica interrupted me, "Oh, yes, I know all about that. I'm really into that stuff."

"So, if it comes to that, I wonder if one of—"

"Oh, I'll come with you."

"That's so comforting to know," I said.

"Do we need to sign anything now?" she asked.

"Jess, I'm not going yet."

Maybe Jessica was a little too excited about the prospect. I'm not sainted like Judy, and I don't know that I deserve it, but I'm so lucky to have my former bandmate for that future date.

Judy's death was the season-three ender. Judy had a triumphant, if truncated, journey. She never became a burden to her family or veered into morose spirals of self-pity when the unknowability of a timeline seemed unbearable, and I just want that progression that I'm bracing for to happen already, before I regain my equanimity. Maybe it takes a THC gummy, a glass of wine, a Klonopin, a meditation, a poem, a GIF of a racoon riding an alligator—or a combination of all those things—to keep moving forward. I'm so grateful for the extra season pickups I've been granted. Still, there's something satisfyingly tidy about Judy's final arc. The next time I get cancer, I'd like to get the neatly packaged sleepy origami kind.

The Happiest Sea Sponge in the Ocean

By the winter of 2023, I'd settled into some semblance of a new normal. Joy was achievable. I no longer felt compelled to respond "still scheduled to die from this" every time someone asked about my health. But sustained mental focus remained elusive. My attention span had become the Mac spinning wheel of death.

In the *before days*, I wrote daily. Sitting down to write has always required heavy lifting. My neighbor John knows that when he sees me cleaning out the gutters on my roof, I'm facing a particularly exacting day. Once at my desk, I'd adapted a version of the Pomodoro Technique, timed writing with short breaks. During these pauses, I'd go for walks, garden, try on dresses acquired before bread and aging left their mark on my midsection to make sure they still didn't fit. I'd award myself decadent treats, slurping down stories on Page Six of the *New York Post*. The mental equivalent of potato chips. One of the surest signs of aging isn't noticeable in any mirror, it's no longer recognizing the subjects of celebrity gossip, but it remained a tawdry pleasure. Queasily satiated, I'd eat actual potato chips before returning to the scraps of notes, piles of notebooks, yellow pads, and loose assemblage of pages that populate my desk.

I'd taken for granted an unfettered access to a well of raw willpower that this process required. It's widely accepted wisdom that when faced with an abundance of challenges requiring your attention, you can simply run out of willpower to continue, because mental energy is as depletable a resource as physical. Thus, the need to institute routines and systems so your daily to-do list doesn't sap your mental energy. Saddled with so many underlying stressors, I was living the depletion dream.

The precision medication—while not causing "chemobrain," which I understand to be far more debilitating—increased forgetfulness and made concentration harder to hold on to. I was leaving a trail of keys, credit cards, and even clothing like breadcrumbs behind me. Words were doing the same thing. After a break, I couldn't summon the willpower to return to where I'd left off. Brain fog is the accepted term. It's like driving a car through thick mist: forward movement is at times impossible. It wasn't exactly a surprise. Everything else required some adaptation. Still, it seemed an unacceptable betrayal by my brain. Et tu, Brute?

Twenty-five years before, the psychiatrist who'd diagnosed me with generalized anxiety and prescribed a selective serotonin reuptake inhibitor (SSRI) had mentioned the benefits of ketamine therapy. Drugs in the SSRI category raise serotonin levels and, if effective, through daily use, can help you maintain a sense of well-being. I'd been walking down Fifth Avenue in New York the moment that SSRI first kicked in and some barometric pressure system inside my head lifted. If life had a soundtrack, "Walking on Sunshine," or something similarly upbeat, would have been blasting. "Is this how other people live?" I thought. That initial euphoria faded, but it gave me a new baseline. With that in mind, and since I was taking a medication that turned off a single cancer-driving gene, might ketamine flip on a willpower gene? Concern over potential long-term side effects had kept me from trying ketamine, but one of the gifts of a stage 4 diagnosis is that that kind of apprehension falls away.

What did I have to lose?

Money, for one thing. The ketamine clinic my psychiatrist recommended cost $675 per session. This was actually a bargain rate. Since ketamine gained popularity in recent years, outlets offering pseudospiritual shaman-led experiences complete with ambient music and atmospheric lighting, the kind of wellness I'd been trying to avoid, have pushed pricing sky-high. This clinic was run by a licensed psychiatrist who could also administer it intranasally to preserve my veins for cancer-related procedures. Armed with letters from my oncologist and psychiatrist testifying to "medical necessity," I pressed my case with insurance. After three denials, I won approval for coverage.

This clinic required a determination of the likelihood of receiving benefits before becoming a client. Two multiple-choice questionnaires, diagnostic tools for mental health disorders widely used in primary care settings, were emailed. These inventories addressed suicidal ideation, irritability, annoyance with others, worry, and lack of concentration.

The surveys instruct you to assign numerical values to your emotional states. Not a stranger to talk therapy, I had no problem explaining my emotional state, but I could have spent the rest of my life parsing the scenarios concerning "quality of mood," which demanded a yes or no answer.

"The mood I experience is very much a normal mood."

Whose normal? Mine? Or normative to the majority of humans using an unspecified metric?

Had I inadvertently been sent a Turing Test?

"Sadness has a rather different quality than the sadness I'd feel if someone close to me died."

What kind of sad are we talking—Motown "The Tears of a Clown" sad? Taylor Swift breakup sad? "The minor falls, and the major lifts" of Leonard Cohen's "Hallelujah" sad?

These assessments elicited the same suicidal ideation, irritability, annoyance with others, worry, and lack of concentration I was trying to mitigate. My score put me in a category of low-level depression, which seemed to disqualify me. Fortunately, the form included a short place to characterize my state of being in my own words. "Diagnosis has triggered feelings of overwhelm and pointlessness," I wrote. An appointment was scheduled with the doctor.

With its anodyne office furniture and overhead fluorescents, the only clue that I wasn't there to refinance my mortgage came when an enthusiastic administrative assistant greeted me with "You're the busiest depressed person we've scheduled!" It had taken some time to wrangle appointments. That seemed a bit off-putting, if also flattering.

I told the doctor I wasn't interested in "tripping."

"Tripping is not an essential part of getting well with ketamine," he assured me. The infusion would cause a temporary dissociative effect, aka tripping, but the long-term aim was a "restabilizing of brain circuitry" when the ketamine was out of the system. He'd had success with other cancer patients. He recommended a trial of six sessions scheduled closely together, followed by reassessment. Many patients scheduled a "consolidation round" of four sessions and then follow-ups as needed over time.

Before each session, my anxiety and depression levels were measured through additional questionnaires. I made an audio recording and took notes afterward.

Session 1

I aced my anxiety test. My score indicated "severe" anxiety.

I am in a windowless but pleasant treatment room painted a soothing robin's-egg blue, seated in front of a painting of a serene sea-glass-green ocean with grassy dunes. The doctor instructs me to inhale, but not too forcefully, to receive the fifty-milligram dosage. He tells me he will monitor my blood pressure, which will rise and then settle to a normal level during the hour we'll spend together.

He warns me that the ketamine will have an acrid taste, which I can offset with a lollipop. He recited the choices of flavors with a near-liturgical lilt: tangerine, raspberry, cherry, grape, chocolate, caramel.

I choose caramel.

Nervous.

"Talking relaxes me," I tell him. Then twenty minutes passes.

"I feel floaty, woozy—like a sea sponge. A collection of porous cells."

Dizzy. Close eyes.

Warmth.

"The grasses in the painting are sucking me in," I say.

"You're not hallucinating," the doctor said. "It's a three-dimensional canvas."

This painting seems ill-advised in a ketamine treatment room, I think, but don't say that out loud.

Numbness. A disappearance of chatter.

I wonder: Am I a character in the psychological thriller *Severance*? Or am I me?

"Do I still have all my fingers?" (Yes.)

"I'm not sure I can stand up again. (I could.)

Jeremy has dropped me off and is waiting nearby. Afterward, I napped. The day continued uneventfully.

Session 2

The mood assessment seems to indicate improvement, but I'd left some of the form blank, instead scribbling in: "maybe less worrying."

Raspberry.

The doctor suggests upping the dosage, but I want to proceed cautiously, so I snort the same fifty-milligram dose.

We are chatting about a painting on the wall—boats moored off a rocky coastline, is it Oregon or Northern California?—when the ketamine kicks in.

Woozy. Sea spongy. Slightly manic cocaine feeling (a remembered sensation from the 1980s).

I am talking about myself. I tell him folksiness annoys me.

"Macramé is triggering."

I ask if he's seen the film *Everything Everywhere All at Once* and describe the plot in intricate detail, something I couldn't do if I weren't high as a kite.

Thoughts are coming faster than usual.

"Do you think ketamine treatment is an extreme thing to do?" I ask.

He does not.

Afterward, I took a nap, continued with my day, essentially unchanged.

Session 3

Instead of filling out the questionnaires, I write, "Having bird by bird issues," a reference to Anne Lamott's *Bird by Bird: Some Instructions on Writing and Life*.

The doctor gently explains that the office staff is "flummoxed" by my refusal to fill out the questionnaires.

Flummoxed myself, and feeling as though I've let the office staff down, I accidentally switch off my recording before receiving the ketamine. My notes are spare.

Back to caramel.

Fifty milligrams.

Sea spongy.

Session 4

Despite my doctor's admonitions, I can't bring myself to fill in the assessment. I leave the majority blank, noting, "Still having looping thoughts but perhaps (I feel) a bit of relief."

Caramel.

We raise the dosage to sixty milligrams.

Twenty minutes in, I am no longer in the treatment room, I am in the 1984 film adaptation of Frank Herbert's *Dune*. Why am I in a movie that was universally panned? In the film, characters ingest a psychotropic substance and have visions of beads of oil dropping into a pool of water. I'm inside the drop. I'm in a shower. The water raining down on me is flecked with gold. I'm swimming alongside my friend Annie in August's tranquil Katama Bay on Martha's Vineyard. I am standing in the sand, gentle waves lapping at my toes.

Or am I the sand? I'm inside a churning tunnel of water. I feel tipsy.

"This is awful," I say.

"Make your way back to calm water," I hear the doctor say, as if from a distant shore on a faraway planet. I'm able to do that, but now my head is a lava lamp. A tsunami-like, blood-orange wave splashes across my field of vision and washes my brain away.

"My looping thoughts have disappeared, but so have all my thoughts," I say.

"I'm not here to get nirvana in a nasal spray," I tell the doctor. But I get it anyway.

"I'm the happiest sea sponge in the ocean," I say. I'm a collection of cells, the water passing through the thin membrane that is my body.

A few minutes pass. My skull, which had melted away, hardens back into a protective shell.

"I don't think I can endure this anymore," I say.

The doctor doesn't upsell me. He suggests I review my notes and circle back.

Session 5

I'd worked so hard to get the insurance coverage that I decide to complete the series.

I've returned to the Oregon coast.

Caramel again.

I snort the sixty milligrams.

"I really don't like the druggy experience," I say. "Does anyone like the dissociative sensation?"

"Maybe some people in their twenties," the doctor says.

When the ketamine kicks in, I feel manic.

"I don't want to be doing this on a regular basis."

Afterward, I nap. The day proceeds uneventfully.

Session 6

Sixth time's the charm?

I hand over the assessment form, the majority of which I've left blank.

The formerly gregarious assistant peers at me from her desk, fixing her gaze on me just a smidge longer than seems comfortable. She brandishes a black permanent marker and inks a large question mark instead of tallying my assessment score.

"I'm not sure if this is enough of a game changer for me to continue treatment," I say as the ketamine kicks in again and my brain puddings. I can't face the administrative assistant. Along with my own goals, I've let the office staff down. I'm a ketamine failure and a jerk.

He tells me that most people, if they are going to feel a benefit, feel it by this time.

"I'm not doing a happy dance, but I'm handling things," I respond.

I am talking too quickly.

"People report that they can take things more in stride," the doctor says.

"I don't enjoy this," I say, when the spongy feeling dissolves the space between me and the world.

I am talking too slowly.

"This will be the last time I see you for a while," he says.

I can't tell if I'm being broken up with or being discharged as a patient.

I ask if he can give me the mood assessment forms for my records. (He can.)

The doctor says he hopes I will see benefits and will check in with me in a few weeks. (He does.)

***

Over the following months, I watched and waited for improvement in my brain function. There was some recovery, but was that a placebo effect, continued acclimation to the medication, or wishful thinking after having invested a significant amount of money and time? I'd also enrolled in a smorgasbord of breathwork, somatic movement, and meditation courses. Like any self-reported survey of healthy life hacks that aren't conducted in a strictly monitored laboratory setting, it was hard to distinguish correlation v. causation in regard to the ketamine.

This wrestling for attention span isn't unique to cancer patients. *Double dying*, I'd called it—the chance of being hit by a bus and having a terminal illness. Similarly, in an era of endless distractions, with the fragmenting attention economy plus the cognitive side effects from treatment, I'd felt *double distracted*.

On a good day, if I treat my brain like I'm toting a soft-boiled egg in an egg-and-spoon race, I can resist the siren song of doomscrolling and surrender to the superior simplicity of Anne Lamott's bird by birding. Other days, I'm convinced I've woken up in The Further, which is the name of the terrifying realm that exists alongside our world, featured in the *Insidious* movie franchise. It's a foggy netherworld inhabited by tortured souls, or, as I think of it, an arts collective on any given Tuesday.

A few months after my failed ketamine experiment, I checked in with my friend Caitlin, who had become a reliable source of dry wisdom, having been in treatment for stage 4 breast cancer for twenty-one years. Early on, I'd called her after someone said, "You've got a cancer personality. You're going to need to examine that before you'll get better."

"How do I make it stop?"

You don't have to say Hail Marys, you don't have to make sacrifices to the gods, juice, or think positively, just take the pills and show up at your appointments, she'd said. Now Caitlin asked if I'd availed myself of the hospital's spiritual counseling. Take advantage of anything offered. It's free! she texted. The image of the Imerman Angels logo flashed in my head; there was no way I was going to delay, as I'd done with my angel. The next week, I was matched with Chaplain Steve, a Jewish, Buddhist, atheist, Juilliard-trained former actor and as close to a soulmate as I've ever come.

Once a week, Steve leads me through a short meditation. The goal is to be able to call up this state of calmness when panic strikes, like when you're having a vasovagal reaction. Sometimes we'll do a little alternate nasal breathing. Hillary Clinton has spoken in praise of this practice, which means that some people will see it as a left-wing conspiracy. Whether you subscribe to it helping regulate the parasympathetic nervous system or not, taking the time to alternate between breathing in and out of each side of your nose is relaxing because at a minimum, you must slow down and think, is this my left or right nostril?

Steve works with dementia patients and people who've suffered brain injuries. He says he's just reminding me of the coping mechanisms I already know, reviving strategies I had at my fingertips, before my fingerprints vanished. Steve loves to toss out words with the prefix *re*. And he's right. I'd studied that kind of breathwork as an actress, and done it for years, but it was another of those life skills that had been raptured.

I compared notes with a twentysomething friend who uses ketamine under medical supervision to treat anxiety, OCD, and depression. The tripping wasn't problematic for him. He, too, had watery adventures, but his had the quality of a babbling brook. He described a "peaceful, liberating, floating along on the current" sensation. After his sessions, he says, "The muck of inaction has been removed, culling the little voice in my head that constantly tells me I'm stuck and will stay stuck forever."

A year after my ketamine experiment, Matthew Perry's death was attributed to a fatal dose of ketamine. He and I weren't friends. We'd worked together briefly and traveled in some of the same circles so I ran into him from time to time. What stays with me was that Perry had an incandescence. Any room he entered crackled with electricity. I wouldn't know why he was attracted to ketamine. My happy place is to be engaged with the world, but I can only imagine that if floating along in the current was Perry's desired state, and that if I had the means, I might do anything to get there again. And again. And again.

A sea sponge is heartless. It has no organs at all, and without a central nervous system, it doesn't experience pain or pleasure, or anything we recognize as sentience, although they can sneeze, which seems like something requiring sentience but doesn't. A sea sponge isn't burdened by comparing itself to others, so it's really not possible to say I was the happiest sea sponge in the ocean. Still, for a very few floaty moments, it was pretty great.

The Wall of No

The Wall of No is not officially recognized as a medical or psychological condition. It doesn't appear on any map, and Google can't locate it for you. But for those of us with chronic conditions, the Wall of No is every bit as existent as the Great Wall of China.

One of the bewilderments of negotiating a life with complex medical conditions is that you find yourself held captive in the tangled web of health care systems. You quickly realize this setup, which you are dependent upon for survival, appears to have it in for you.

Remember HAL, the artificial intelligence running the spaceship in *2001: A Space Odyssey* who decides humans aren't as important as his own self-preservation? Everything you encounter when managing a chronic disease reminds you of HAL's famous line, "I'm sorry, Dave, I'm afraid I can't do that."

Before I even dealt with my medical issues, a potluck of legal documents needed updating: wills, beneficiary designations, advance care directives. This is where the humor of the damned provides last-resort relief. *At least I won't have to slog through applications for long-term care insurance, because no one will sell it to me now* is sometimes the only bright spot of the day when I'm drowning in paperwork.

Add to this the Kafkaesque—I'm required by the internationally recognized rules of patient engagement to invoke Kafka—combinations of billing statements, new claims, incorrectly processed claims, the inevitable claim refilings, logic-defying denials, brain-breaking appeals, and the sacrifice of your firstborn that you must attend to in order to satisfy the accounting services of your care teams. One of the telltale signs you're in for a protracted journey is when you graduate from a single doctor to a care team.

I maintained a five-alarm-fire readiness, but despite close to around-the-clock vigilance, construction of another expanse of the Wall of No had already broken ground.

Try as I might, my sensible attempts to have my care provided under one roof fell flat. The hospital where my oncologist practiced was in network, but a specialist I needed to see, at that same facility, was not. A designation could change overnight with no notice, and you'd find out only when it appeared on your explanation of benefits.

On one occasion, I woke up to find that my insurer had withdrawn $4,333 from my checking account. I'd enrolled in a patient-assistance program, and between that and my insurance, the cost of my Tagrisso, the miracle drug, should have been entirely underwritten. Having a reliable system in place to avoid such a costly scenario had been essential to my mental as well as financial health. Another error by my insurer caused a domino of effects. I was told that because I had an unpaid balance of $5,363.23 for the Tagrisso prescription, I couldn't order a refill for my antianxiety medication. Only, there was no unpaid balance. A pharmacist at a local, family-owned store where I'd been a customer for twenty years was generous enough to bridge the gap. You know who really needs their antianxiety prescription refilled? A person in treatment for stage 4 cancer.

The mind-numbing attempt to correct the mistakes and have the funds returned to me took countless emails, phone calls, and some amount of crying. In the process, I discovered that an additional layer of bureaucracy had been added to the procurement process of my medication. I had been unaware because the name of this new third-party entity appeared nowhere on any documentation, and I'd dismissed the "onboarding" call I'd received as spam.

"Hi, this is Unintelligible Name from SaveOn."

"Who? I don't use Sav-On Pharmacy."

"We're not Sav-On Pharmacy; we're SaveOnSP, a specialty pharmacy." SaveOn was pronounced exactly the same as Sav-On, just to be more confusing.

"I just changed insurers," I said, "and I've been in close contact with my new plan."

"Yes, and we're your specialty pharmacy's specialty pharmacy. If you don't sign up with us you'll be charged the full amount of your co-pay of $4,500 every month for your specialty medication. We have all your information. You just have to verbally consent to let us manage your account."

"Okay?" I replied. Was there a real choice?

It sounded like a Mafia shakedown out of *Goodfellas*. I promptly forgot about the call and received no paperwork. An explanation for these errors was not forthcoming. Insurance companies follow the same code of conduct as Tinder daters: expect ghosting. You'll never receive an apology, much less acknowledgment of a mistake made by the offending party.

In researching an op-ed that I published in *The Washington Post*, I learned that as treatment with precision meds became more widespread, health insurance companies hired shadowy third parties to deal with the very highest tier of medications, including the biomarker targeted therapies indicated for lung cancer.

Even more troubling than my accounting snafus were other policies that affect millions of us. These third parties had decided that if they didn't want to apply the contributions made by patient-assistance programs, like the one from which I was receiving underwriting, to a beneficiary's out-of-pocket payment obligations, including deductibles and out-of-pocket maximums, they were free to act as they saw fit. This allowed insurers to collect twice, once from the patient-assistance programs and then again from the patients. In financial schemes, this kind of thing is what's called "double-dipping."

Here's how it plays out in practical terms: If my cousin Rena contributed $20,000 to the cost of my medication, that amount would count toward my deductible and out-of-pocket maximum, so why should funds designated specifically to assist me, just because they come from a pharmaceutical company, not also be applied to my deductible and out-of-pocket maximum, as well?

If that sounds confusing, it is. If that sounds like a predatory practice, it is. If that sounds like an illegal practice, it is, but a court has yet to hold them accountable.

In the *before days*, I'd entertained the idea that it was the irresponsible who allowed themselves to be unprepared for medical emergencies. The kicker: I'd counted on being grandfathered into lifetime coverage through one of my union health care plans, an earned benefit accrued from many decades of employment. But because of rising health care costs, the union had ended that benefit just prior to my diagnosis. It made sense to me now that one-third of all GoFundMe campaigns are launched to cover unexpected medical expenses.

It seemed an added cruelty that patients were unaware that it might take them longer to meet out-of-pocket expenses as the ins and outs of their policies were already leaving their heads spinning. How would Nadia, a lung cancer patient I'd met through my expanding advocacy community, deal with such accounting errors? Nadia enjoys the socializing aspect of her job as a server, but she takes bar orders from the back of a golf cart at a country club, so how could she spend hours on customer service holds as I'd had to endure?

As a kid, I was always getting gum stuck in my long hair. My mother used to work peanut butter into the snarled sections until the day she got fed up, took out scissors, and started snipping away.

Cutting out this middleman in health insurance wasn't an option. In hopes of becoming that informed consumer our politicians routinely suggest Americans need to be, I investigated switching insurance plans. Two years had passed since the pulmonologist had asked if I had a good insurance plan and urged me not to make any changes. I'd thought I'd understood why, but I hadn't had the entire picture. Now I faced the Wall of No transparency: Because precision medications fall outside standard (outdated) pharmaceutical formularies, companies aren't bound by law to inform you what your medication will cost before you sign up, thwarting the possibility of performing due diligence in insurance shopping.

In the summer of 2023, I took a hard look at my finances. I was shelling out $1,200 a month to keep the best insurance plan, and the bodywork to ease the medication-related muscle pain was not reimbursable. Despite my relatively low overhead, I was spending down my savings to meet expenses.

Stabilizing my finances by applying for disability benefits, essentially collecting Social Security early, and taking early retirement from my union seemed like something I should consider.

With a shorter anticipated lifespan, it might make sense to pull the trigger; what was I waiting for? On the other hand, preserving benefits at the maximum level could be wiser because I might live longer than originally predicted. During the relatively short time since I'd been diagnosed, better prognosticators for which patients could expect longer tenures on the miracle drug had been confirmed. Patients like me, who'd started treatment before the cancer metastasized to the brain (one of the first places it typically spreads) and who don't have detectable cancer markers circulating in their bloodstream, on average, got longer. With that in mind, it might make sense to wait on the pensions and Social Security. Only, I was working less and without a steady income, so I might run through my savings.

I recalled something noted thoracic oncologist David Carbone had said to me. He'd told an early-stage patient, "You're cured!" and she'd said, "Oh, shit, I spent all my money."

Einstein showed us that time is relative, but this doesn't have anything to do with how we actually experience life. It might be because I live in California, but I've lost count of how many times someone has said "time isn't linear" and "the past, present, and future are all informing each other." I'm dubious that these people have stared down the list of income reported from the year they entered the workforce, scrawled their parents' age at death next to the survival rate of their life-threatening disease, multiplied (or maybe divided?) the penalty percentages incurred for each year of collecting Social Security and their pensions before normal retirement age, and calculated that giving up thousands of dollars a month was the right course of action.

Time's arrow was pointed in one direction.

A word I'd glimpsed hovering so far on my distant horizon that it shimmered like a mirage, sped toward me, solid. I rolled its hard consonant around my tongue like a sour lemon drop: pensioner.

If someone tells you hordes of fraudsters are hijacking government benefits, this is an indication they've never applied for disability. The wait time to get a claim reviewed when I called Social Security was 220 days, and that hadn't accounted for the impact of an anticipated slashing of 12 percent of the workforce in 2025.

I was required to have a call with a Social Security official. I got dressed up, just as I had for my initial telehealth diagnosis Zoom, even though I wouldn't be visible, as a way of marking the significance of the day. I wasn't retiring, exactly. I could continue working (you can continue to work part-time when on disability), but I was acknowledging something I already knew but hadn't wanted to put into words: I would never have the same level of output. Also, once you begin collecting Social Security, that decision can't be reversed. I'd be forever forfeiting the greater amount I'd worked for and looked forward to with anticipation over the years, even if I stopped collecting disability. No backsies.

I sat glued to my chair, afraid to miss the call.

I was reminded of the time I'd not only gotten dressed up, but also cleaned my apartment in preparation for a phone call from Martin Scorsese after auditioning for a role in *The Last Temptation of Christ.* I hadn't gotten the role, and it was extremely considerate that he'd taken the time to call me. That news moved the dial as I'd been weighing a decision to move to Los Angeles to pursue employment in television.

This call would potentially usher in a new chapter of my life as well.

I thought about my lung cancer community around the globe, all of whom weigh these same kinds of decisions each day, calculated bets on our lifespans, amateur actuaries all.

"Every happy family is alike; each unhappy family is unhappy in its own way," Tolstoy wrote. Surely his genius was intuiting that this sentiment would be portable to the point of ubiquity. Everyone is uniformly happy to be alive at "the best time in history to be diagnosed with lung cancer," as my second-opinion oncologist had said. We take hope from the scientific advances that each month bring us more options for treatment and inch us closer to a cure, but the Walls of Nos we encounter are as varied as the bagels at Zingerman's Bakehouse. Some have been served the everything bagel.

I'd weighed this decision with Lysa B., as she's known in advocacy circles. She and I were introduced at an event held by the Lung Cancer Foundation of America, a patient advocacy group. Lysa was the first person I met in treatment, and she was gracious enough to become my go-to person after Hardye died. We've split restaurant checks and vacationed together. Now, on scan days, I check in with my sister, Lisa, and Lysa. She'd also been told "we'll do the best we can, for as long as we can." That was fourteen years ago.

Lysa went from a career as a highly skilled radiology technician to volunteering fifteen hours a week at an animal shelter. Full-time work wasn't sustainable; neither was standing on her feet all day. Now she's retired. She's weathered a series of TKIs, surgeries, radiation, drug trials, and is living the joyful future she'd never imagined for herself: She's a grandma and is pursuing her love of art and crafting. She has lobbied Congress for lung cancer funding and is a participant in a promising drug trial, traveling once a month from her home in Florida to Tennessee to receive a treatment that has kept her cancer at bay for two years. These trials contain significant risks for the participants and the results inform treatment for the global population. It's really a form of public service. She flies home the same day, as there's no budget for hotels.

She purchases her own plane ticket, which is reimbursable, but there have been times when it's taken five months to get repaid. At one point, the reimbursement was months behind, and she and her husband were sweating out a $4K check they were owed. This is an example of the indirect costs of drug trials and also why lower-income individuals are statistically unrepresented in trials. Lysa gets an allowance of seventy-five dollars a day for meals, only it's broken down by meal, and she can't eat prior to treatment and is home by dinnertime, so she can use the twenty dollars the study allocates only for lunch. She buys the same sandwich at the airport each time she flies. Her chicken salad wrap costs $21.34 plus tax. That extra four dollars on each trip impacts her monthly budget, so she never buys a beverage, a piece of fruit, or a bag of chips.

As we in the United States continue to delegate more health care authority to individual states, inequities increase. Meanwhile, EU residents, as well as citizens of Iceland, Norway, Liechtenstein, and Switzerland, and NHS patients in the UK (not patients in a private system), can receive ongoing care in another EU country, with the cost, other than travel, covered by their home country's health care system. The sharing of resources means faster treatment routes for patients and the opportunity to receive treatment that might not otherwise be available. I hadn't known this until I overheard a French oncologist at the 2025 World Conference on Lung Cancer talking about how his clinic has patients from across the continent. Countries with universal health care have their own peculiarities—there's a longer and more stringent review process for medications to become standard protocol since the cost will be covered for all citizens. Still, I was stunned. Ongoing care coverage administrated through Medicaid isn't transferrable.

State by state in the U.S., "the best time in history" is conditional. The average five-year survival rate for someone with stage 4 lung cancer in Alabama, where I was born, is 16.8 percent, but in California, where I live now, it's 21.5 percent. Our health care system privileges state autonomy, so each state administrates Medicaid differently. Those who took what was termed the Medicaid expansion, at the onset of the Affordable Care Act, mostly cover biomarker testing, while those that didn't, for the most part, don't. Medicaid covers genetic mutation testing in North Carolina, but just across the state line in Tennessee, it doesn't. And if you live in a location where you're not provided with testing, you might never be told about biomarker therapies. This affects not only lung cancer patients, but people with all sorts of conditions.

Many don't get the treatments, even if approved for genomic testing. Due to lack of access in rural areas, only one in five Medicaid patients in the state of Alabama get the miracle drugs even when their cancer has the EGFR or the ALK biomarker (also prevalent in colon cancer), two common lung cancer mutations.

There are also brilliant outposts in some of the most challenged spaces. In 2024, I visited the University of Alabama, Birmingham. They're piloting a virtual tumor board and sponsoring monthly online meetings in which specialists volunteer their expertise to assist rural doctors in underserved communities around the state.

In many parts of the Global South, precision medications aren't accessible except to the very wealthy, so the gradations of "the best time in history" are extreme.

The phone rang. I didn't wait the two rings that I do for business contacts to demonstrate that I am a very busy and in-demand professional. A potential pensioner needs observe no such etiquette. I began crying when the Social Security claim specialist came on the line. With this call, if I got the part, so to speak, I'd be ushering in another new chapter of my life. The staffer asked a question to square the date I'd filed for disability with income I'd declared.

When I answered, he burst into tears. "I read your case and I was hoping to avoid telling you that you owed back taxes." Oh, no, I broke Social Security. I was both touched and worried for this kind soul's continued employment. Surely, this job would destroy him if he cried during each interview? If there was a silver lining, it landed like a slap to the face: Late-stage lung cancer is one of the handful of diagnoses that get automatic approval. They expect you to die before costing the system too much. We had a good cry and wished each other luck.

In addition to stabilizing my economy, on December 26, 2024, a class-action suit for which I'm the lead plaintiff was filed against SaveOnSP, LLC, Express Scripts, Inc., and Accredo Health Group, Inc. That case is pending in the United States District Court for the Western District of New York. My hope is to help millions of patients save money. You can't scale the Wall of No. You can't dig under it or catapult over it. But you can chip away at it. One predatory scheme at a time.

Tiny Victories

It started in the *before times* with a story I couldn't stop thinking about.

On Sun, Nov 17, 2019, at 11:21 AM, Barbara Ehrenreich wrote:

> *Here's my latest. Comments welcome!*
> (link: *The Humanoid Stain: Art lessons from our cave-dwelling ancestors in* The Baffler Magazine)

On Nov 23, 2019, at 10:48 PM, Annabelle Gurwitch wrote:

> *Oh, what a joyous and terrible look at the progression of our species—from prankster artists to selfie-taking planet destroyers. So many things to ponder. Thank you so much for this gift of thought, hilarity, and break from the horror of the day.*

On Nov 25, 2019, at 8:17 PM, Barbara Ehrenreich wrote:

> *This obsessed me for over a year. Even now I can't let go and find myself strangely drawn back to the Paleolithic, which of course accounts for most of our species' time on earth. . . . My big news: I'm going to be a grandma for the 3rd time!*

This kind of mash-up of cultural criticism and everyday life updates was typical of my relationship with Barbara. Her mordant wit elevated my spirits and our discursive exchanges improved the quality of my thinking, and that giddy astonishment at having lucked into friendship with such a brilliant person, who also had a soft spot for comedy, never waned. She was a compadre and a mentor to many writers, though I'm sure would have scoffed at that second label.

For the next six months, what had been her obsession became mine. In "The Humanoid Stain," Barbara challenges widely accepted conceits about the cave drawings in Lascaux, France, and, by extension, thousands of paintings from that era. Since their discovery, the drawings have been seen as symbolic "of a time when 'man had just emerged from a purely zoological existence, [and] instead of being dominated by animals, he began to dominate them.'" And yet, she argues, the contrast of the supernatural attention to facial and muscular detail of the megafauna versus the humans who appear as faceless bipedal stick figures demonstrates an acute perception of their lesser importance. "Maybe," Barbara reasons, "in the ever-challenging context of an animal-dominated planet, the demand for human solidarity so far exceeded the need for individual recognition that, at least in artistic representation, humans didn't need faces."

It had long been assumed that paintings were done by Jackson Pollock Paleolithic Era lone artist types, but newer studies have proven they were created by highly organized groups. This, Barbara argues, points to the value our relatively ego-free ancestors placed on community. Lastly, writing on the meme-likeness of the drawings, she tells us that their creators—who "didn't even bother to sign their names"—were sending communiques between communities: "Here we are, creatures like yourselves, and this is what we know."

If "we're better together" was buried in our epigenic code, then perhaps as a species we aren't doomed. Wasn't her reconsideration a sort of redemptive vote, though a tiny one?

As important as her actual investigation was that instead of seeking self-care through spa days, retail therapy, or day drinking, Barbara's escape from selfie culture and the sense that "narcissism [had] been democratized" involved throwing herself "down the rabbit hole of paleoarcheological scholarship."

The essay buzzed my brain in the best way possible: I'm a person for whom pedagogical debates are like mainlining Red Bull. How had I forgotten that? I read it over and over, studying her reasoning, marveling at both form and content.

I spoke about the essay at dinner parties, emailed links to friends, shared it on my socials, buttonholed strangers at the dry cleaner's into discussions of cave painting. Maggie, my writer friend with the Zen practice, was at one of the dinner parties—it was actually at her house, so I basically held my host hostage with "The Humanoid Stain." She, in turn, countered by redeeming the much-maligned human tendency, for which I am woefully guilty, toward gossip. "Gossip is derived from *godsipp*, an Old English term," according to Maggie. "God mothers, the women folk, would gather together and gossip as a way to discuss values of the culture." Confirmation bias or another tiny victory? My mind started racing. Others might be hungry for this. Maybe this was fodder for a podcast? But this was the last thing I wanted to do. At that time, in 2019, everyone and their sister was starting a podcast. I was sure my cats were plotting their own podcast while I slept. Did the world need another podcast? Maybe it could be a tiny podcast? Maybe fifteen minutes long?

I recruited comedian Laura House into this enterprise. We'd met eons ago. I'm not keen on these designations, but I'd met Laura through my ex and I *got her in the divorce.* We'd never collaborated, much less made a lunch date, but I was a fan. In her solo show, *How to Hate Yourself,* she skewered self-help seminars while being authentically uplifting, a deft magic trick. I'd started thinking of the show as a kind of practice, though that term seemed overused to the point of meaninglessness. Laura occasionally teaches meditation classes, which I'd attended, and her nonprecious approach seemed like the right ethos for the show.

We'd found a home with the Maximum Fun podcast network, founded by Jesse Thorn, the host of *Bullseye*, a pop culture podcast carried on NPR, and were refining the idea with network producer Laura Swisher when the pandemic hit. Now our focus shifted. Enlivening stories would be useful, but we decided to focus on celebrating minor accomplishments and fleeting joys, the only successes available at a time when getting out of bed each day felt like a triumph. We'd invite listeners to call in and share wins: A *Tiny Victories* Hotline! The name was intended to poke fun at the urgent need to affirm the achievement of the inconsequential. We hoped that someone might call in to report something like . . . they'd survived a three-hour customer service hold, a hotline call we would later, in fact, receive.

We were still developing the show when my life went zombie apocalypse. Now no one needed to look for succor of the spirit more than me.

After delaying to accommodate the months of testing, we launched in November 2020 with Barbara's Paleolithic story.

Maggie's gossip story was included in our third episode. There were times when I'd need to reschedule with as little notice as announcing, "I have to take a nap" in the middle of a taping. The Lauras' patience was repeatedly tested during that first year, as I was in such a fog that I missed recording sessions and was chronically late. The pandemic meant we needed to record at home, and despite Swisher's tutorials, I was in the throes of peak brain fog and couldn't retain the sequential instructions to use GarageBand or the Zoom recorder the network lent me, and I needed to relearn these skills over and over. Somehow, we managed to get this soupçon of a show off the ground. Another tiny victory.

The goal was to provide small rescues, but not take ourselves overly seriously. In one episode, I described a class I'd been sitting in on. My teacher, Rich Panico, talks about art and meditation over Zoom. He's the teacher who issues the reminder that "you are the sky; everything that happens is weather." He opens each class by reading an excerpt or a short poem. Twice. The first time he reads, I have an inner monologue going: *I can't believe I'm listening to poetry. I'm not sure I even like poetry*. But then, during the second listening, my brain focuses, and I think: I love poetry, poetry is amazing. I wanted to share this experience and I was sure that Laura would be a convert, but when I described Rich's method, without missing a beat, she said, "That sounds awful." So, without planning in advance what her reaction would be, I played a recording of Rich reciting Mary Oliver's "Wild Geese." Twice. Laura paused. *Here it comes*, I thought, ready to celebrate my tiny victory. "Nope, still hate it," she said.

Each week, we invited our listeners to put "a pause on their anxiety" and share "one thing that gives us a reason to get out of bed." Our topics wound up touching on many of the strategies I was adopting. In one episode, "Sad Songs Help a Little, Not a Lot," we explored the death humor that my friends and family found disconcerting.

I'd taken to playing, on repeat, a song from a musical by Young Jean Lee, which Bart had recommended.

The play is called We're Gonna Die. You can find a video online, Bart texted.

Are you sure I want to see this? I replied.

Trust me.

Five minutes in, I discovered that the show was about dealing with the death of her father from lung cancer.

You do know that her dad dies of lung cancer? I texted.

Give it a chance, darling, Bart texted back.

I did.

The podcast was a good excuse to have a conversation about how diving straight into the darkest feelings produces joy. In the episode we recorded, I explained to Laura that Young Jean Lee frames the play by saying she's going to tell a story about the worst thing that happened in her life. She says, "A friend of mine sent me a letter to cheer me up," and so I expected to hear a song about how it only gets better, what I'd call a chin-up, cheer-up song. And then the song starts . . .

Who do you think you are? / To be immune from tragedy? / What makes you so special? / That you should be unscathed.

She continues.

Horrible things happen all the time.

It was like an exorcism. I played the song over and over, I danced to it around the house, and suddenly this weight turned into lightness. And the best part, the reason it felt like a tiny victory, is what she says in this next part of the song.

That's when I sing a little song / That makes me feel a little better / Just a little / Not a lot.

Finding things that help us just a little, not a lot. By the end of the play, she had the entire audience clapping along with her and singing . . .

I'm gonna die / I'm gonna die someday / Then I'll be gone / And it'll be okay.

(excerpted from the podcast)

Laura

I love that this tiny victory is rooted in sadness, because it seems like something we would try to avoid. In my meditation, I've learned you actually just have to sit in this stuff; we can't avoid the third of emotions that we just don't like. You can't just pick your top five emotions and be, like, I'll just feel these.

I have never gotten a bigger response on social media than when I announced that we were recording a show about sad songs. "September Song" by Kurt Weill—but only the Lou Reed version—"Total Eclipse of the Heart," Death Cab for Cutie's "I Will Follow You into the Dark," Alejandro Escovedo's "About This Love," anything by Nick Drake. I asked Laura if she had a favorite sad song.

Laura

Gosh, I thought of so many, but my current one is Lewis Capaldi's "Before You Go." He sings about wishing he could have done something to help someone he loved. When you hear it, at first, it sounds like kind of just another breakup song. There's a longing and an ache and pain. Then you learn that his aunt, I believe, [died by] suicide. And that's what the song is about. Like, could I have helped you? Even thinking about it, like, I start to tear up. And here's another reason I love sad songs. I think it's the opposite of Anna Karenina. She's, like, everyone is happy in the same way, but sad is specific. I think we're sad in the same way. I was at an outlet mall a couple of weeks ago, and I'm in the restroom and cackling teenage girls come in, and that song came on, we entered a reverie. Me and these teenage girls who are worlds apart, we didn't want to sing, but we kind of were singing, complete strangers. We were the same: We love people and we feel pain.

Annabelle

That's interesting: how in grief, we're all the same. There's a lot of science about how music lights up the neural pathways in your brain. There was a study done recently at the University of Limerick, which is a place I would have liked to have attended, because then I could say, "Oh, yes, I went to Limerick."

Laura

There once was a girl in college. She went to get her some knowledge. She studied at Limerick . . .

Annabelle

Do you know how much they must hate that? They must be like: *We get it, it's a rhyme, we've heard every Limerick joke.* But they did a study there that showed that when feeling down, the majority of people reached for a sad song, not something to change their mood. Because what it does for you (whether you're aware or not) is it helps you process the emotions, which helps you move on, and also put things in perspective.

Laura

Yay, sadness!

From October 2020 through November 2023, once a week, Laura and I bridged the space between "I can't go on and I'll go on," one tiny victory at a time. We had some thousands of listeners per week, like Young Jean Lee's song, we had "a little (following) not a lot." We recorded 200 episodes. It felt like we'd achieved our goals for the show, including adjudicating the eternal debate over whether the pumpkin spice latte represents a value-adding evolutionary adaptation or is a precursor of the end times. One of the last episodes we recorded was a paean to Barbara's arresting intellect and trailblazing life.

From: Barbara Ehrenreich
Date: Sat, Mar 12, 2022, at 4:39 PM

Subject: Oh no!

Just read your cancer piece in the Washington Post. *Did you tell me months ago and I was just too distracted by my own peculiar illnesses to keep it in mind? Because my reaction was: wow, this is the friend I need right now! Why haven't we been in constant contact? So much to talk about, like the incredible ageism of medicine. My advice for getting through treatments is to bitch and moan all the way through. Let's cheer each other up or at least vent. Make an appointment for a call. Soon.*

I didn't call.

Nickle and Dimed is Barbara's most widely read book, illuminating the life of the often invisible workforce that powers our society. Her passing in the same week as Labor Day 2022 seemed somehow appropriate.

It was a huge loss for me not to get to bitch and moan with her, but with Barbara's health declining, I didn't want to risk putting her through that. Some of the hardest calls had been with teachers, mentors, and friends a few years my senior. It was upsetting for them in the way that you don't want your children to suffer.

I missed my chance to commiserate with her, but I teamed up with Alissa Quart, Barbara's close friend and cofounder of the Economic Hardship Reporting Project. Working with the resourceful staff at Symphony Space in Manhattan, we produced a tribute hosted by Pulitzer Prize-winning journalist Maria Hinojosa and that featured readings by Broadway stars and cultural commentators. Afterward, I heard audience members exclaiming, "I always loved her work, but I hadn't remembered how funny she was."

After recording our last episode, we received our final Hotline call.

Final Hotline Caller

> Hi, I wrote down on my to-do list "Tiny Victories podcast" many times, and I finally found your podcast, and I love your podcast and thought "these are my people." And the very first episode I found is the one where you announce you're ending the podcast. So, my tiny victory is: It would be so like me to say, "You suck that you didn't find the podcast a long, long time ago." But I'm rising above it, and I'm just telling you that I will enjoy listening to the past podcasts. I love laughing with you. Thanks for everything. Bye.

I couldn't have thought of a more appropriate note to close out our run.

We ended the podcast, but each time I remember to look for tiny wins, my day is better for it. I was at a conference of lung cancer survivors in May 2025 when someone brought out a white (that's the dedicated lung cancer color) ribbon the size of a kindergartener for us to pose with. Previously, in such situations, I'd made it a point to announce my prohibition to the three R's: no runs, ribbons, or religion. One of the lessons I've taken from the cognitive dissonance of looking unaffected was a daily reminder that I never know what others are going through. So maybe it was really meaningful for this person to have us all hold the ribbon. In the photograph, you can see that we're all so happy to be together. Some of those in the picture have become close friends. We're wearing lanyards with badges from the conference. They are adorned with colorful add-ons: *I'm here for the drinks. Goddess. Plays well with others.* If you look closely you'll notice that I've made my own. *Keeping Cancer Bitchy!* I'm holding the ribbon, smiling, and still bitchy. A tiny victory.

Blossoms

It's always April at my home. Eternally spring. Mentos-sized opalescent blossoms cascade unendingly, some might say relentlessly, on the patterned wallpaper I had installed in my guest bedroom.

The vertical motif mimics a waterfall. I often lie on the bed staring until, *Matrix*-like, the buds morph into streaming 1s and 0s, spraying upward like a digital fountain, heaven bound. It is probably best not to partake in psychedelics in this room.

This wallpaper was a gift from a friend with fabulously extravagant taste. Let's call him Seamus. Seamus produced a film I acted in twenty-five years ago. We'd stayed in touch intermittently, but when, a decade later, he moved within walking distance of my home, we discovered shared interests: slow-cooked meats, obscure literary works, and vintage textiles.

Wes Anderson, with his meticulously detailed interiors, would have a field day with Seamus's bold design choices. The wallpaper in Seamus's dining room is stunning in its verdant lushness. Flower heads the size of baby hippos, pistils akin to Viking spears, ferns you could park a tank inside. The palette of shadowy greens, bruisy browns, fleshy pinks, and bloody reds has emotional impact. Think Rubens's *Massacre of the Innocents* if the theme were power struggle in the floristic kingdom.

His daughter's bedroom was papered with blossoms. The background of the paper is blue—not a babyish *Blue's Clues* blue, but a sophisticated blue with gray undertones; a blue that the Pantone Institute color wizards call Dutch blue; a hue I find invigorating and soothing: the hot chocolate of blues.

Adding to the appeal is the texture. Unlike the plasticky vinyl of my 1970s childhood bedroom—chosen because "it's the easiest to wash," the salesperson said, accurately pegging me as a here-comes-trouble kid—this paper had granular fibrousness.

"I have extra rolls. Take it," Seamus said over dinner at his place, during the early days in my *after life*.

"Are you sure?"

"What am I going to do with it? It's old, so you'll need someone who knows what they're doing. I have a guy."

"Of course you do."

Seamus is that person who always has a guy or knows a guy who knows a guy. Even if the guy is a woman, she's a guy, and Seamus knows her.

Back home, I unfurled a roll. I ran my fingers over the thick paper's frayed edges, placed my nose close to the surface and sniffed. It didn't have scent so much as density. It smelled substantial. I promptly deposited the rolls in a cabinet, where they remained for three years. Thus began my annual observance of UOP: Unfurling of the Paper.

What was I going to do with wallpaper?

Wallpaper, vintage or otherwise, signifies the ushering in of a new era. You hang it when you move into a home, when renovating for the birth of a child, or when that child leaves the nest. Not when you're a ticking clock.

Also, I'd heard that vintage wallpaper installation is pricey. Expensive interior design has never figured into my discretionary budget, which at the time was devoted to moisturizers to repair the damage my medication was wreaking on my skin. Making it even harder to justify was a stipulation, from my Zoom divorce, that I sell the home at a future date that loomed ever closer. Another ticking clock, added to the one already counting down.

Along with my post-diagnosis wobbliness around decision-making, there was also the memory of a dubious design choice I'd made *before* cancer: the ill-fated tricolor paint scheme in the guest bedroom. Inspired by an article on how color blocking could add dimension to a small space, I'd envisioned a subtle but statement-making motif of muted radish, celadon, and a warm cream. The paint colors I purchased were closer to stop-sign red, Lucky Charms leprechaun green, and tighty-whitey. I painted it myself.

"Why is this room the colors of the Italian flag?" I'd been routinely asked for over twenty years. Change comes slowly when you're on a budget.

Four years into treatment, during my ritual Unfurling of the Paper, I flashed onto the contents of one of the care packages my grandmother Rebecca sent during the last years of her life. The contents were either items she intended for donation to Goodwill, mistakenly sent to me, or things she thought might come in handy. I never asked because I didn't want to know the answer. A package might contain: an open box of aspirin, the brocade dress she'd worn to my bat mitzvah, an expired can of tuna, three spoons, a signed copy of an Isaac Bashevis Singer novel (which I treasure), and a set of new pillowcases (practical). Once she sent an extension cord. It was neatly wrapped around a piece of cardboard, a beaten-up top to a Tiffany gift box. She'd made a notation on the box top, whose distinctive robin's-egg patina is trademarked Tiffany Blue. *Saving this in case I ever get another home of my own—Rebecca R. Gurwitch.*

My grandmother was living in a modest apartment by that point. She was never going to own another home.

Saving this in case I ever feel my decisions are trustworthy enough to commit to anything that speaks to permanence—Annabelle Gurwitch.

I envisioned my son finding a handwritten note when cleaning out the cabinets after my death. No. My penmanship is so illegible I'd have to type it up and print it out.

There was never going to be a right time to hang this wallpaper.

"Hey, Seamus, can you connect me with your guy?"

Two weeks later, Peter, Seamus's guy, set up an elaborate workstation in the room. This had been my son's playroom, really a toy storage area, then my office, my ex's office, then his marital "purgatory" bedroom. After we split up, it became the bedroom I rented out to help cover my mortgage. I'd taken the "we'll do the best we can for as long as we can" call there. I'd been avoiding it ever since, as if the room were somehow complicit in the diagnosis. Was this an elaborate attempt to reclaim this space? Maybe, but I'd also priced out the installation and I could afford to paper only one wall.

During the two days it took Peter to hang the wallpaper, he told me he'd learned how to hang vintage paper, made more difficult by its fragility, from his grandmother in Georgia—the country. He told me that he was an actor and encouraged me to watch his reel, which I never did out of fear that whatever talent he displayed could not possibly be more engrossing than his pre–industrial revolution skill set. Watching him reminded me of *Raboteurs de parquet*, the floor scrappers, by French Impressionist Gustave Caillebotte.

Three men are kneeling, their muscular arms extending with the effort of scraping the veneer of a wooden floor in a Paris apartment. *Raboteurs* was notable at that time for Caillebotte's depiction of urban laborers, but I just like the muscular bodies of the workers, the dancerly quality of their movements, and how the sunlight reflects on the floorboards. Peter's craft demanded a similar amalgam requiring painstaking concentration. The brittle paper needed careful trimming. A wheat paste adhesive was applied with a small brush and smoothed onto the drywall with a wooden hand-rolling tool, antediluvian in appearance. I had to resist the impulse to award him a standing O.

Once the paper was up, I experienced that universal post-design-change mania: Now the entire house needed updating. I should wallpaper all the walls in my home. I should do the ceilings. I googled: "Is wallpapering floors a thing?" I needed more of this paper.

One of the bonuses of assigning yourself a project like researching vintage wallpaper is that it provides a focal point for any stray anxieties. So, down the rabbit hole I went, following the trail of clues from markings along the edgings of the paper.

My pattern, "L'Avril," is archived on the website of the Thomas Strahan Company, founded in New England in 1866. The exact date this wallpaper was produced was impossible to ascertain, as numerous versions appeared over the years. My paper bears the stamp of the United Wall Paper Craftsmen of North America (UWPC), founded in 1923, so the paper postdates that time.

A deeper dive revealed that the brushstrokes on the floral patterns, like those on my paper, were inspired by Chinese and Asian textile designs. It's a style called chinoiserie, which roughly translates to Chinese-*ish*. In the mid-eighteenth century, a chinoiserie room was installed in Buckingham Palace, and the style became popular with the masses, reaching its height in the 1920s and '30s in America. Its popularity has continued—Anthropologie and Ralph Lauren offer chinoiserie designs.

Had cancer turned me into an accidental Orientalist? At least, I consoled myself, my paper wasn't one of the more egregious of chinoiseries—patterns that exoticize Asian life with ethnically stereotyped figures, exaggerated eye shapes, and landscapes lousy with dragons and pagodas. Except, some of those dragons and pagodas looked awfully familiar.

A quick look around my house woke me up. I'd lived for so long, with so much, I had stopped seeing it. My house is filled with Asian-*ish* objects that my mother, a frequenter of auctions and antiques outlets, collected. I have a Trader Joe's selection of porcelain altar fruits: mangos, apples, pomegranates, eggplant, Buddha's hands. Ginger jars, plates, tureens, painted tiles, an enamel fire screen, the ashtray I keep keys in by the front door, the mason jar with the Q-tips in the bathroom.

I was the poster child for chinoiserie.

This is what can happen when we research provenances. That's why it's a good idea to think twice before sending in that saliva for 23andMe.

The revelation produces the worst kind of ethical queasiness, the kind where you know you're compromising your ethics, but you don't want to have to change your actions and you're looking for any way to square not having to address your participation.

"Do you think Mom knew she had chinoiserie?" I asked my sister.

"Oh, definitely," she said. "Remember how we used to joke that she could recite the dynasties and not our schoolteachers' names?"

I didn't, but the benign neglect of my latchkey childhood suddenly made more sense.

I found an essay by Aileen Kwun in *Elle Decor* titled "It's Time to Rethink Chinoiserie." She writes: "a decorative design object is never just an object. It is a stand-in for what is valued." Chinoiserie, she writes, should be viewed as a kind of chop suey. The American idea of Chinese food in the 1960s.

It got worse. Traditional American patterns like L'Avril have become co-opted as "cottagecore," a style trendy with the tradwife set. Had cancer turned me into a trad wannabe? This is a digital-era spin on Phyllis Schlafly's happy homemaker mythology meets florid fantasy of pioneer women's lives. The tradwives of TikTok toil away at their wifely duties, spending as much time on eyelash extensions as they do on promoting their lines of sunscreen made from scratch, a product no one needs to DIY and that dermatologists have roundly dismissed as dangerously ineffective. Decked out in prairie dresses, they perform their Stepford Kabuki in front of cottagecore wallpaper disastrously similar to mine.

In an attempt to cull the herd, I tried to ascertain items' authenticity and monetary value. The altar fruits were of Chinese origin, but assorted jars, dishes, and that fire screen with its enamel pagodas and dragons? Those were troubling. An intricate hand-painted plate appeared to be Japanese, from the Meiji era (1868–1912). It might be worth several hundred or several thousand dollars. Or, not. It might be a knockoff. My mother kept no records and she amassed these artifacts during both the lean and flush years of my childhood, so the only way to thoroughly investigate would be to engage an auction house. Even if I lived another fifty years, that wouldn't give me enough time or mental energy to go down that path.

"Annabelle, don't sweat it. No one loved chinoiserie more than the Chinese. My home is full of it," my friend, the writer Sandra

Tsing Loh assured me when I presented my dilemma to her. That was a welcome vote of reassurance.

My mother was an inconsistent presence, but the tchotchkes she collected during my childhood provide the comfort of continuity, and I'm not giving that up, especially now.

Because I'm a terrible person, I fantasize about a future in which my son is saddled with these same objects. He's showing a friend the vast array of chinoiseries he inherited from his mother on the floor-to-ceiling shelf, custom-built to accomodate them in his 200-square-foot apartment. "The thing is I have no idea if she knew what this was or if it had any value, but she was such an important person in my life, I can't let go of them."

It's been April in the guest room for almost a year now. What was I waiting for? Well, disposable income, there's that. The cost was not enough to make a difference in my future, but it vastly improved my present. The room is now my sanctuary: The repeated pattern acts like a visual mantra. I also love the word that the paper introduced me to: inflorescence, the flower head of a plant. How did I ever live without that word?

When you visit my home, I will show you L'Avril. I will tell you not to delay in instituting small gestures that add beauty in your life. I will tell you not to make your own sunscreen. I will tell you the checkered history of chinoiserie.

Just don't tell me that I've gone cottagecore.

Laurels

It takes a security guard and a chain-link stanchion to protect Bernini's *Apollo and Daphne* from being pawed at by overzealous art lovers like me, so I'm fangirling it, pressing in to get as close as possible without risking arrest. It's May 2025, and about as perfect a morning as I've ever experienced even in my *before life.* I am in Rome—what could be bad about that? I've had exactly the right amount of caffeine, and the sun isn't so strong that I need to drape myself in my Bedouin-inspired coastal grandma garb. I am with a cherished friend I rarely get a chance to see—if you consider communing with a sculpture a coffee klatch, which I do.

Apollo and Daphne, completed in 1625 and considered one of Bernini's finest, occupies center stage in a domed chamber in the Villa Borghese. Opaque shades obscure the view of the villa's gardens, allowing only a satiny muted light to filter in through lofty windows. Spotlights are trained on the sculpture, adding to the drama and focusing our attention. Unlike other galleries with multiple focal points, there's no mistaking that Apollo and Daphne are the headliners.

The milky white marble has an undulating liquidity, as though the figures have been poured into corporeality. The bodies are curvy and supple but have a tautness like chilled butter. Apollo's calf is deliciously within reach and I'm tempted to lick it.

The Borghese limits the number of daily visitors, so to gain admittance, most of those present, including me, have signed up for guided tours. The groups advance from room to room, swarming the big-ticket attractions—other Berninis and paintings by Caravaggio, Raphael, da Vinci, and Titian—but I've ditched my tour and ducked into this gallery as another group tramps on.

I first became acquainted with *Apollo and Daphne* during a 2022 visit to Rome. Since then, Daphne had supplanted Persephone as my Greek mythology It-girl.

Bernini's sculpture was inspired by the Greek god Apollo's unrequited lust for the maiden Daphne. With Cupid as wingman, Apollo was stalking Daphne. Daphne was, like, not okay, Cupid. A wood nymph, she delighted in solitary forest walks and fording streams and wasn't interested in hookups. Nevertheless, Apollo was determined to possess her.

The sculpture sees Apollo in pursuit, hot on her heels. The folds of his robe billow like sails in strong headwinds. His thighs are sinewy, evincing his powerful stride. Their bodies are mere inches apart, his hand encircles her waist. In desperation, Daphne called out to her father, Peneus, a river god: "Help! Father! If these streams of yours are holy, destroy what makes me pleasing. Change my form!" (Stephanie McCarter's translation of *Metamorphoses*). Her prayer is answered.

Bernini depicts the instant Daphne is transformed into a laurel tree. Bark, like a knobby, rough-hewn plaster cast, shoots up from her ankles, overtaking one of her thighs, threatening to encase her torso. Her fingertips sprout veiny leaves. Her ropey locks fly wildly, framing her face. Her arms are outstretched, her mouth a gaping expression of horror. Think Sissy Spacek's Carrie-at-the-prom pig's-blood betrayal.

Emotionally intense and action-packed, sculptures of the Baroque period—unlike Michelangelo's *Pietà*, a Renaissance masterpiece—were intended to be viewed from all sides, so I circle *Apollo and Daphne* in contemplation, as though walking a labyrinth.

On my first visit to the Borghese, I'd seen something of myself in Daphne's plight. The cancer occupying my lungs seemed an invading army akin to her zombie conversion. The desire to harden as a means of survival felt familiar. The anguish of metamorphosis—hers and mine—seemed to unite us.

I'd come to Italy in 2022 to speak at the winter gathering of the Rome chapter of Women Against Lung Cancer in Europe (WALCE). This invitation came after delivering an opening address at the 2022 IASLC World Conference in Vienna. After the publication of the *New York Times* essay, I received a slew of invitations. Initially, I'd balked. I didn't want to become a professional sick person: *Annabelle Cancer.*

So I'd said yes to every request.

I was uncharacteristically nervous in Vienna. I'd given hundreds of talks and lectures, walked the high wire of live television interviews, but the stakes didn't quite register until my arrival at the convention center. I'd known there would be thousands of oncologists in attendance, but the sheer crush of stakeholders, including other patients and representatives from every major cancer center in the world, was intimidating. Plus, many thousands more would be tuning in to the live stream from home. I was addressing the very people I was counting on to save my life. What if I alienated them in some way and got added to a "No Treat List" like the "No Fly List"?

I'd begun preparing, as per usual, months in advance, but was still revising fifteen minutes before the ceremony was set to begin. I rushed into the cavernous hall with newly printed pages in hand.

I'd been warned that humor might not translate to this audience, but I'd decided to go for it. Because . . . comedy gal. For the first few minutes, you could hear a pin drop. Feigning a vasovagal event seemed like a good idea.

When I suggested that if Ben and Jerry could come up with the ooey-gooey goodness of Chunky Monkey, which is both a cookie *and* an ice cream, someone should be able to concoct a more flavorful version of that sickeningly sweet iodinated solution we are required to drink before scans, audience members clapped and even hooted. I spoke of my tenure as a Merch Crone, the Persephone-like dual world existence of facing long-term treatment with unknown timelines, and how I'd shown photographs of my son to radiography technicians in hopes of them becoming invested in my continuance above ground.

A lifetime of stage experience did not prepare me for the vulnerability I felt as I reached my concluding remarks. When a standing ovation came, I teetered and almost fell from the podium. That was when Silvia Novello, an esteemed Italian thoracic oncologist, swooped in, took my arm, and whispered, "You must come to Rome." As I hobbled offstage, I said, "Yes. I must come to Rome."

Afterward, a gaggle of oncologists shepherded me to the annual bash, where I danced until almost hyperventilating. Midnight came and went, and though there were early-morning sessions the next day, these folks were still going strong. What drugs were these doctors on? I was hailing a taxi when some of those same scientists and surgeons insisted that I join them at a late-night watering hole.

"You do remember, I have this disease, right?" They weren't budging.

And then it occurred to me that if anything were to happen, I'd be fine. Because . . . doctors. "No, you're dead," one of them said. "We're so highly specialized, we'd be completely useless to you!" I almost laughed up one of my cancer-riddled lungs and off we went.

The next morning, thanks to zwei double espressos Viennese style, I got up to attend a 7 a.m. plenary. I'd been a C-minus science student, so I was fortunate to have Brendon Stiles, chief of thoracic surgery at Montefiore Einstein Comprehensive Cancer Center, accompany me. A conference photographer snapped a shot that still makes me smile when I look back on it. I'm leaning in to ask a question of Dr. Stiles. Despite being masked, you can read in my expression an eagerness to learn. However, the hunch of my shoulders and arch of my eyebrows communicates something else: I'm entirely out of my depth. I'd had the sensation my brain was stretching, like salt water taffy ribboning.

That morning, I learned there was a proven link between the targeted therapy that was still holding my cancer stable and the UTIs I got regularly. Turning the EGFR gene off, the gene that had gone rogue, causes skin degradation (extreme dryness), so it makes sense that along with the outer layer of epidermis, the skin inside the vagina would suffer as well, making for a bacteria-friendly climate that leads to UTIs. Attention had simply not been paid to this type of side effect. As Jack West, another longtime thoracic oncologist, explained to me, "When the only treatments available were highly toxic and debilitating chemo and radiation, sex wasn't top of mind for doctors or patients either." That my oncologist—a leading practitioner at a well-regarded institution—was unaware of the connection was troubling, but also an example of how quickly the science moves. As of 2025, two-thirds of those diagnosed with lung cancer in America are nonsmoking women under fifty years of age. This epidemic volume drew thoracic oncologist and associate director of the Cancer Care Equity Program at Dana-Farber, Narjust Florez, to specialize in addressing the needs of this population, which included issues like mine. Seventy-seven percent of those queried in her Sexual Health Assessment in Women with Lung Cancer (SHAWL) study reported treatment-related sexual dysfunction.

When it came time for questions, I rose from my seat. "My dry vagina and I thank you so much for what you're doing." To many of those gathered, I will always be "the vagina lady."

The conference was an awakening. IASLC has one of the most innovative training programs designed to prepare patients and other stakeholders for collaborating with researchers, doctors, and health care institutions. Some of those in attendance had successfully lobbied for comprehensive screening initiatives in their countries of origin. Others were making vital contributions to the development of treatments by prioritizing patients' needs in their reviews of proposals for trials and studies. They were addressing the existential dilemma Hardye had faced and many of us were urgently facing: QOL, or quality of life, concerns versus OS, or overall (length of) survival. They had me at help for my vagina.

The Rome conference took place a few months after Vienna, and was primarily a community-building event for patients. Among those in attendance was Patti, who co-founded ALK Positive, a European patient advocacy coalition, to better support her husband in treatment for ALK, another form of oncogene-driven lung cancer. We exchanged stories over a drink. Paolo, her husband, had been cajoled into taking the waters at Lourdes, an old-world iteration of the Quantum 360 Center. Pilgrims have sought healing there since 1858, when a fourteen-year-old peasant named

Bernadette Soubirous claimed to have had eighteen encounters with the Virgin Mary. Paolo hadn't been cured, but the friend who accompanied him, a true believer, was diagnosed with lung cancer upon their return. If I'd written that as a movie script, audiences would think I'd made it up. It was also confirmation of our many shared cross-cultural experiences.

In what has to be one of the best cancer card plays ever, we were granted a private tour of the Vatican. That evening, a group from the conference, fifty in number, were ushered into the Sistine Chapel. I lay down on one of the benches and peered heavenward. When Ezra was a baby, people said he would have gotten a lot of modeling work in Michelangelo's time, with his angelic face and shock of curly blond hair. Now I saw something familiar in the profile of the fourth cherub from the right, just peeking out from behind God. But then, doesn't every mother see her kid in that mural?

Jeremy had accompanied me to Rome in 2022. He'd attended my talk, as had Jessica and her husband, Adam, who serendipitously were in Italy. Inviting Jeremy and my friends into this world tested my "need to know" boundaries; they'd see me in an environment where my primary identification was as a person in treatment. The memory of sharing this experience is indelibly, achingly, intimate, but the most satisfying feedback came via Patti. I'd spoken of how essential it was to my survival to preserve as much normalcy in my life as I can for as long as I can. Paolo had been watching a live stream from home. He'd been an avid cyclist prior to his diagnosis, and once I said that, he shut down his computer, suited up, and headed out for a ride. I couldn't have imagined in the *before times* that someone tuning me out might be the best measure of successful messaging.

The following day, Jeremy and I had visited the Borghese, and that night, the American Academy in Rome, which is located on eleven verdant acres on the Janiculum, the second highest hill overlooking the city. Toni Morrison, artist Kara Walker, playwright Lynn Nottage, and Alice Waters, among others, have spent time there—it's a convivial, nerdy paradise. In 2022, Marla Stone, a writer friend, was serving a term as the administrator. Over drinks in the Academy bar, we fell into lively conversation with various scholars and artists-in-residence. "You should apply as a visiting scholar next year," Marla said. "I will," I answered, by which I meant, "I won't." I wasn't making plans that far in advance.

Three years later, thanks to the mentoring of more experienced patient advocates and medical professionals, I am one of those patient advocates who understands the jargon and speaks the language. I rate myself a solid C-plus science student. I collaborate on studies, serve on multinational, multidisciplinary faculties of several organizations, and publish on a variety of survivorship issues. In this community, everyone knows the odds, no one minimizes the stakes, and hope, delicious food, and collegial competition are the steady fare.

A personal benefit of patient advocacy is the exchange of informed advice. At one of the world conferences, a scientist, who'd become a confidant, said, "You know, Annabelle, you might be around for a while. This might be a good time to rethink your care team." I'd joked that my oncologist's lack of eye contact was comforting in its own way. "If he didn't think it was important to engage directly," I'd said, "maybe my case of lung cancer wasn't so dire after all." The scientist and I had been sharing drinks, but her comment was sobering. I understood that she was reflecting on the way that personalized medicine had precipitated changes in the paradigm of the doctor-patient relationship. With so many new trials and drugs in the pipeline, we were encouraging patients to participate in shared decision-making. Maybe I needed to take the advice I'd been giving others? She was acknowledging that the time would come when choices would need to be made. She gave me a doctor's name, Ravi Salgia, the chair of medical oncology at City of Hope. This would have meant changing hospital systems and that was more upheaval than I was prepared for at that time.

Meanwhile, I'd heard great things about a well-regarded female oncologist who'd recently been recruited to my hospital. Perhaps we could work on the UTI issue, and then I'd return to my regularly scheduled appointments with my oncologist. I'd grown accustomed to his open-grave tone-deaf assessments, or maybe I was used to rejection from my years as an actress. Because she practiced in the same hospital, scheduling an appointment with her required a referral from my doctor.

It turns out it's a lot easier to speak in front of thousands of people than it is to speak up when you're alone in an exam room sitting opposite one doctor. I took a full year to work up the courage to say, "I'd like to get a second opinion."

"I don't think your case is worth her time," my oncologist said. I'd appreciated his air of indifference, but I didn't want confirmation of actual indifference. I left his office, my face burning with shame and anger. I couldn't recover from that.

Now I was going to have to switch entire care teams. At my first appointment with Dr. Salgia, he assured me that every single case was important to him and that he was keeping a close eye on the latest advancements. He would let me know the options when the appropriate time came.

"That's not going to work for me," I said. I was looking for that more nuanced dialogue.

"Annabelle, what you're addressing is the Epimetheus and Prometheus dilemma." Epimetheus, Dr. Salgia explained, was Prometheus's lesser-known brother who was always playing catch-up, while Prometheus was always looking ahead. If following a Promethean path, you'd be inclined to take more aggressive measures, acting prior to a patient showing progression. That path risks becoming ineligible for yet-to-be-discovered treatments. If Epimethean, you're stuck playing whack-a-mole, but you haven't closed any doors you might need to walk through. There'd been a recent sea change in thinking and many thoracic oncologists who'd been solidly in the Promethean camp were trending Epimethean. We'd have an open dialogue. He had me at Epimetheus.

An upside of switching systems and leaving the Ian Schrager–like boutique hotel hospital behind is that there's less temptation to steal art.

Along with changing my approach to my treatment, I was using my accrued knowledge with my mentees, which is why even as I was recovering from the lumpectomy, I wasn't going to miss the ASCO conference in Chicago. And as if I needed more confirmation that the arc of the universe bends toward irony, at a conference dinner, I was seated at a table with my former "I don't think your case is worth her time" oncologist. I'd thought of many things I'd wanted to say to him since leaving his care, none of them repeatable, but that's not what came out of my mouth when I sidled over to him.

"Your prediction came true: I've lived long enough to get diagnosed with breast cancer. I just had a lumpectomy. It is the best time in the history of the world to be diagnosed with lung cancer, at least for someone with access to the new drugs." His health was holding stable, as well. We toasted to both of our continued survivals with glasses of fine wine. Finally, the fine wine he'd prescribed.

In the years since the Rome conference, I hadn't stopped thinking about Daphne. At first, Daphne's transformation represented a normalization of death as a returning to the earth. I'd researched tattoo designs with the plan of having night jasmine climbing up my arms, inked in delicate pastels, but I nixed that idea. There were enough needles in my life.

Now, three years and another cancer later, I was back in Rome. I'd sweated out the Academy's application process and no one was more surprised than me to be there. My residency at the Academy represented an important milestone since my "shipwreck of the soul." With no existential wobbliness, I'd made a decision. Whether my scans revealed progression or not, I would travel to Rome for a three-week residency. If necessary, we'd wait until my return to start whatever plan B came next. Dr. Salgia and the team signed off.

I had worrisome incidents in the interim. Respiratory infections have become more frequent, and after one bout, I'd needed supplemental oxygen for a few hours each day. The wheezing sound of my home oxygen compressor seemed to portend poorly to a return to Rome. Fortunately, I recovered enough for an inhaler to suffice when my breathing becomes labored. The stability provided by my disability benefits and pensions allowed me to feel less anxious about the costs incurred. I'd applied with the goal of contemplating metamorphosis and mortality in the eternal city, and I was doing just that.

Apollo and Daphne's faces are unlined, and their limberness suggests youthful locomotion. Of course, I'm almost three years older than when I first glimpsed their dazzling physiques, and although my background-level fatigue is rarely perceptible to others, suddenly even ancient statuary seems exceedingly spry.

During my earlier visit, I hadn't noticed that while Daphne is barefoot, Apollo wears sandals. Even the leather as rendered in marble looks expensive. And how had I missed that flex of his wrist in my first viewing? Apollo's expression is poker-faced placid, but that wrist is a tell that he's aware something out of the ordinary is happening. In Stephanie McCarter's translation of *Metamorphoses*, Apollo notes Daphne's "loose, disheveled hair." He wonders, "Suppose that it were styled!" Did Stevie Nicks have Daphne in mind when she cooked up Rhiannon? Always, always keep it witchy, unruly, for as long as you have hair, I tell myself.

I take my last looks. My tour has arrived, and even though I've extended my stay to six weeks, my days in Rome are limited.

I have writing waiting to be edited, that is, between checking in on the live-feed cam at Jackie and Shadow's nest. After that devastating loss in 2023, the Big Bear bald eagles finally had chicks. The local kindergarten class in Big Bear gets naming rights and I check in on the eaglets, Gizmo and Sunny, at least once or seventeen times a day.

I've fallen behind because it takes me longer to write, and, despite that, I left work unfinished last night to meet up with Patti and Paolo. They have a regulars' spot at a bar near their home, within walking distance of the Academy. I was elated to be reunited. Paolo is eight years out from diagnosis and already planning a ten-year blowout cancerversary celebration. Like me, he's remained stable on his TKI. He's still cycling, but he left a position as a high-level business consultant that he'd worked for years to attain. He's secured new less-stressful, more-manageable employment, but the loss of identity and hit to their finances is something they are dealing with, another cross-cultural experience.

At my desk in Rome, I found a review of the 1981 Beckett production of *Texts for Nothing*. "Let's see what happens next," the reviewer quotes as the next line following "I can't go on, I'll go on." How could I have forgotten that? My copy of the text doesn't include that line, but the production was an adaptation of several works. I might have saved myself some time had I recalled that invitation, but like chaplain Steve says, I'm remembering things I've forgotten.

I'm also preparing, while in Rome, for my next visit with Neena and Jessica. Ukes will be involved, but we haven't revived Flowers for Algernon. Along with inspiring her to find her voice, *Fiddler* sparked Jessica's founding of the Campfire Project, with its theme of displacement and diaspora. Neena and I have joined Jessica's assemblage of artists and mental health counselors to create theater, music, visual arts, and dance with young migrants seeking asylum. Our therapeutic arts programming not only fulfills my love of teaching young adults, but is another Stammtisch for our throuple.

Campfire encourages a 1970s communal, help-in-whatever-way-is-needed, hippie ethos, so my tenure as support staff for DPS has come in handy. This is how I wound up assuming the position of assistant song leader with Sudanese refugees in the West Nile Valley, where, in addition to singing all day, I discovered the addictiveness of unleavened chapati.

Who am I kidding? I came to Rome for the mandel bread. Jeremy and I had this specialty of Boccione Bakery's on our 2022 trip. He's arriving tomorrow and I plan to surprise him. In my "second life," with less paradigm-shifting consequences than Matisse with his cutouts, I continue to try out new things that don't have associations with my former self. I prefer "I'm deeply, deeply fond of you," which is a phrase I've never said to anyone, instead of "I love you," which I've said too many times. Jeremy has been gracious enough to have a sense of humor about my fondness for fondness.

On the advice of another resident at the Academy, I've graduated from my clunky, stilted high school *Metamorphoses* to Stephanie McCarter's stunning recent translation.

Ovid, McCarter explains, "explores the innate fragility of the human body, how subject it is to the forces beyond our control, and he recognizes how traumatic such lack of agency can be."

And yet, unlike the other transformations in Greek mythology, Daphne exercises agency over her destiny. The Gods punished mortals for moral and ethical transgressions with demotion: from human to animal and even human to object. There are many such comeuppances in Greek mythology: Dionysus turns pirates into dolphins; Zeus turns Io into a cow; Hera turns Echo into a disembodied voice; even Demeter—my favorite mother figure—turns a young boy into a gecko. There's something to be said for Daphne's asserting herself, even to the limits of her power, a mythological modeling of "volitional affirmation of the obligatory."

Perhaps congratulations were in order for her. Trees, with their vast supportive networks, might represent an upgrade. If you have to transform, and change is inevitable, a laurel tree isn't the worst-case scenario. I, too, have grown some bark, some emotional armor, to survive.

I slip out of the gallery quietly, before the first tear lands on my cheek.

It will take me a while to get from the Borghese to Boccione Bakery due to my stubborn insistence on traversing the city without consulting the internet. The detours, backtracking, the meandering through lesser-known parts produce that ego-free cousin of the wander: the sonder, that liberating anonymity of being the background to other people's lives. Boccione, on the other hand, is world famous for their twist on a traditional almond biscotti. Burnt on the outside, chewy on the inside, it's perfect in its own way.

Ultimately, McCarter writes, "*Metamorphoses* [. . .] helps us reflect upon our own (in)humanity, our vulnerability, and our capacity for change."

Apollo and Daphne is also perfect, and I think it could use a little improvement. *Daphne and Apollo* would more accurately reflect the hero of this myth. And, as much as I enjoy each detail of her horror, I'd like to see what happens next: Daphne's curiosity as she embraces her capacity to change. Just as I am curious about my own capacity to change. I'm not curious about pain, but I am curious how I will deal with the pain that my future likely holds because I am a big baby. Daphne's example is one we could all aspire to. Let's not forget, the laurel wreath we honor athletes and recent graduates with are Daphne's lasting legacy. A tribute to her triumph.

As for my Daphne, the Daphne I'm becoming? Well, she wouldn't have to smile, exactly, at least not a toothy grin. Maybe that *Mona Lisa* smile? Look how I'm transforming. It makes me grin myself to think of it. If you should read that someone has, let's not call it *defaced*, rather given Daphne a glow-*up*, but the perpetrator's identity is unknown because no fingerprints were left, well, you'll know who was responsible.

Afterword

I'm not a doctor, nor have I played one on TV, but if you or someone you love has been diagnosed with a life-altering condition, here are a few tips, strategies, and resources that have been helpful to me.

1. World Wide Web of disinformation

Your doctor might say, "Don't go on the internet," after which you'll immediately sign on to the internet. Dr. Google is a fickle friend with a less-than-reliable relationship to facts. Ask your doctor or the nursing staff for a list of vetted sources. When I was diagnosed with stage zero breast cancer, I was handed a packet of useful information, but I wasn't offered any direction to find resources when diagnosed with lung cancer, and had I known to ask, I could have saved myself a lot of time and trauma from exposure to random internet info.

Look for nonprofits and 501(c)(3) charitable organizations with medical advisory boards. If something sounds too good to be true, it is. Run the name of organizations where you are getting information by your medical provider's office.

If you are tempted to try an alternative cure, tell your doctor first. It might be contraindicated even if it isn't on a list of drug interactions. While many oncologists aren't cheerleaders for supplements that are untested, they've heard it all, and you don't need to apologize for trying something, just exercise caution. One of the ways to protect yourself from quackery is to look for someone who is FABNO (Fellow of the American Board of Naturopathic Oncology) certified. Also, to recognize science from speculative treatments that sound science-based, you'll want to check that the studies and data have been peer reviewed. And before purchasing any speculative, expensive healing technology, let's take a trip to Paris instead. I know a great hotel.

2. We all need support.

It's okay to need additional support beyond your family and friends. Many wellness gurus offer community, but most of those will cost you money. Lots of it. Most patient support organizations can direct you to support groups for patients and caregivers that meet online or in person at no cost. Facebook is currently a great resource where nonprofits host moderated private groups in which members share experience, strength, and hope. You can also join anonymously.

Because many of the groups are multinational, you can reach out just about any hour of the day for support. The moderators at EGFR Resisters Lung Cancer Patient Group, my home group, post links to newly announced trials and peer-reviewed studies from vetted sources, and members post mitigations for side effects that are often helpful. There's a saying in 12-step programs, "Take what you like and leave the rest," and this applies to these groups as well.

Someone is bound to post something annoying, but don't let that stand in your way of getting the benefits.

If you're looking for one-on-one mentoring, Imerman Angels is one of many nonprofits that matches individuals with the same disease. Many institutions offer ongoing counseling either with their team of social workers or through their chaplaincy services at no cost to the patient. The chaplain I meet with regularly has experience with oncology patients and these sessions are invaluable. There are also therapists who specialize in counseling people in treatment. It is not an admission of weakness to need extra support.

3. Too taboo for you?

If you feel uncomfortable addressing any issues you're encountering with your doctor during your regularly scheduled appointments, consider reaching out in a different way. For some people, email or a telehealth appointment is an easier way to ask questions. Also, you might seek out someone else on the staff—a nurse practitioner or another office staffer you feel comfortable with—and ask them for guidance.

4. Ask questions that open productive discussions.

We want responses to our concerns: reassurances, time frames, facts, plans of action, and hope. But we don't always have the language or a shared decision-making process in place with our provider. In a video series titled "No One Missed," sponsored by the LUNGevity Foundation, Dr. Jorge Gomez at Mount Sinai offers a helpful prompt: "This is what I want, can you help me get there?"

I recommend this to my mentees, and I have found it useful myself. It can be applied in navigating complex decisions for any condition.

I've adapted it to: "This is my goal; how close can you get me to achieving my goal?" I prefer "how close" because at the moment, what I want is a cure and that's not possible at this time.

Goals can look very different. One of my mentees had a very specific idea of how she wanted to live. R was in her early fifties and wanted to retain a normal quality of life for as long as possible. She didn't want to reveal to her employer that she was in an ongoing cancer treatment. Thanks to having an actionable biomarker mutation, she was able to achieve her goal pretty seamlessly, with the exception of a few bouts of intense side effects. Then in 2022, a trial found that adding chemotherapy to her targeted therapy could increase survival time. After weighing the benefits, which amounted to a few extra months, she decided that it wasn't worth being tethered to an infusion schedule and the lingering side effects of chemo.

Others in our community have made the opposite choice. One of those patients, Laura, was significantly younger, and had young children and religious beliefs that drove her decision-making. She wanted to throw everything at it, even if it meant her quality of life was severely impacted, to try and stay alive long enough to see a cure.

Sadly, patient advocate extraordinaire Laura Greco died in 2024. Personalized medicine has given us more choices but this means there are no simple answers. Hence, open and nuanced communication is key.

5. You are your best patient advocate.

6. We're speaking the same language, but I can't understand a word you're saying.

If you've had any experience with the medical world, it's not a surprise that its lexicon can seem impenetrable or even punitive.

In the chapter "The Coronavirus Saved My Life," I write about the extreme gastric event that led to my son dubbing me Cancer Mom. It wasn't until I saw a presentation about a new drug trial that included a toxicity scale for measuring gastric side effects that I understood the extent of the communication gap between provider and patient. What I experienced at the start of treatment fell into the category of severe to life-threatening, but I hadn't known what was considered tolerable and what might be considered extreme. Also, I was so relieved to not be on traditional chemo that I didn't want to complain.

It wasn't until thoracic oncologist Narjust Florez said to me, "Patients think they need to suffer; we can help with that," that I understood it was acceptable to speak up for myself. When setting off on a treatment, it's perfectly reasonable to ask your doctor what kind of scale she is using to measure toxicities. And, as if a patient needs one more responsibility, by giving your doctor honest feedback, you'll be helping the next patient.

Here's an example: One of my mentees was experiencing a disfiguring and painful rash. Her doctor said, "I have patients whose rash is worse than yours." That wasn't helpful. By advocating for herself, she was able to get her dosage reduced with good results. Typically, doctors prescribe the dosage that has been shown effective in clinical trials, and often that's the highest tolerable amount. There is a movement to rethink this and start treatment at the lowest dosage that effectiveness has been measured. Patients experiencing unmanageable side effects often discontinue treatment that might otherwise be beneficial when started at a dosage they can't tolerate. You can read about one of these efforts, a patient-centered dosing initiative led by breast cancer survivors, at the website TheRightDose.org.

7. "Help me help you" and the three H's communication strategy

The classic Tom Cruise/Cuba Gooding Jr. scene in *Jerry Maguire* holds up, and it's very relatable in dealing with the kind of challenges resulting from medical crises. It's disquieting to listen to someone you love going through a hard time and feel powerless to solve their problems. And it's frustrating to be a person going through a difficulty while people suggest things that aren't actionable or appropriate for you.

Having been on both sides of these conversations, my sister and I have adopted the three H's communication strategy: "Would you like a hug, to be helped, or did you just want to be to heard?" If the answer is "hug," then I can respond in a way that affirms the experience instead of rushing to tell someone exactly how to fix their life, which is my first instinct.

8. To get a second opinion or not to get a second opinion? That is the question.

A second opinion can often lead to better outcomes, not to mention greater peace of mind. But before changing doctors, a good idea is to manage expectations by examining what it is you're looking for in a medical provider. Is it bedside manner? Is there a lack of expertise in your condition? Do you feel unheard when voicing concerns? Do calls and emails go unanswered? Are you asking for something like assurance of a cure that's not a reasonable expectation?

Compromises have been involved in all the changes I've made. For example, the hospital where I received care for the first two years in treatment provided scan results on the same day. The hospital where I currently receive care isn't staffed to offer that. However, the total care they provide was worth the change.

Don't hesitate to ask for a second opinion at any point during treatment. A good doctor won't feel threatened by your inquiry. As Dr. Ray Osarogiagbon, who trained as a thespian before turning to oncology and leads the thoracic oncology department at Baptist Memorial in Memphis, told me, "If the second opinion corroborates the first opinion, it gives patients confidence in the plan. If not, it creates an opportunity to reconsider. If your doctor says no to a second opinion, you should get a different doctor."

9. Cancer warrior or cancer slacker: a strategy

I've been asked, "Is this just a joke?" Yes and no. I am both poking fun at this label and serious about taking it on.

Prior to my diagnosis, I'd found warfare metaphors useful. I imagined *getting cancer* to mean something like a marauding army had invaded your body and was holding your spleen or whatever organ for ransom. Cancer as an occupying enemy force. I can only imagine if you are facing an excruciatingly painful treatment regimen that it might be heartening to feel you are gearing up for a battle. I also appreciated Christopher Hitchens's take on it. In *Mortality*, he writes, "I'm not battling cancer; it's battling me."

At the same time, for those of us facing long-term if not lifelong treatment, performative wellness can feel punishing. "Would it hurt you to smile, sweetheart?" is something almost every woman has been subjected to walking down the street. "Yes, it might hurt me to smile today" is my response. Being labeled brave and a fighter on days when those attributes are beyond your capacity can backfire into feeling like a fraud.

Ibrahim Cissé, my Los Angeles neighbor, MacArthur Genius awardee, and director of the Department of Biological Physics at the Max Planck Institute of Immunobiology and Epigenetics in Freiburg, Germany, introduced me to another framework of thinking. Ibrahim says, "Cancer is just cells who have forgotten who they are and we have to help them remember." I consider this approach a détente with my body for what seemed a betrayal. The kinder, gentler language has been an invitation to proceeding with calm detachment, which has been my priority as an anxious person.

Also, ideally, I'd like to expend as little energy and attention on my treatment as possible. I never felt motivated to run a marathon before cancer, and this is one aspect of my identity I decided was worth preserving. So, November 6, 2022, I celebrated my birthday at the New York City Marathon with friends, including pal Triparna Sen, PhD, a cell and molecular biologist and the director of the Sen Lab at the James Cancer Center at Ohio State University. We cheered as the marathoners sped past while we enjoyed coffee and croissants at a bakery along the route.

10. Financial guidance and resources

If you were going backpacking, you'd pack a host of emergency supplies in case of unknown developments, and if it turned out they weren't needed, you'd probably still feel good about having taken precautions. Safety first. But when we're diagnosed with chronic or serious conditions, we often can't imagine the range of impact we will experience, from the immediate and unplanned expenses and loss of income to what kind of planning will be helpful down the line. Most hospitals and cancer centers have financial navigators who can direct you to resources that assist with issues ranging from help with affording groceries to more nuanced issues like strategizing underwriting for expensive medications or mitigating costs associated with clinical trials. Before launching a GoFundMe campaign, for example, you'll want to become aware of the implications this can have on accessing governmental help.

I was aware that others had more pressing financial needs and couldn't imagine that I might benefit from a navigator because I had an accountant and a financial adviser. As it turned out, the people in my orbit weren't experienced with issues related to receiving disability insurance and other kinds of needs that arose. I made missteps that have had unintended long-term consequences.

Experts in financial toxicity recommend establishing contact with financial navigation services at the start of treatment. It's a worthwhile investment of your valuable time and you can also delegate this interaction to someone in your support network. Outside help can be accessed at any point in treatment but you'll need to research that yourself.

My friends at the Lung Cancer Foundation of America have helped me assemble a list of reliable organizations that offer guidance and assistance for many kinds of long-term conditions. You'll find a list of resources via the QR code below. Scan for bonus content and more.

Works Referenced, in Order of Appearance

Naomi Klein, *Doppelganger*, references to Emilio Uranga (Farrar, Straus and Giroux, 2023)

Jenny Odell, references to Georges Perec, "What Happens When Nothing Happens" (*Time*, 2023)

Georges Perec, "Approaches to What?" (*Cause Commune*, 1973)

Jack Flam, *Matisse: A Retrospective* (Park Lane, 1988)

T. S. Eliot, *The Wasteland* (Hogarth Press, 1923)

Katherine Mansfield, *The Diaries of Katherine Mansfield* (Edinburgh University Press, 2016)

Emily Dickinson, "There's a certain Slant of light" (1861)

Elaine May, "not dead, just resting," *Ishtar*, 1987 movie starring Warren Beatty and Dustin Hoffman

Thornton Wilder, *Our Town* (Perennial Classics, 1938)

Ann Patchett, reference to having been an Emily, *Tom Lake* (HarperCollins, 2023)

Kate Bowler, *Everything Happens for a Reason* (Random House, 2018)

Samuel Beckett, *Stories and Texts for Nothing* (adapted by Joe Chaikin, 1981) (Grove Press, 1994)

Works Referenced, in Order of Appearance

Joan Didion, "We Tell Ourselves Stories in Order to Live," *The White Album* (Farrar, Strauss and Giroux Classics, 1979)

Stefano Montali, "The Secret to Deeper Friendships Is in Your Calendar" (*The New York Times*, 2024)

Mihaly Csikszentmihalyi, *Flow: The Psychology of Happiness* (Harper & Row, 1990)

Otto Rank, *Art and Artist* (W. W. Norton & Co., 1989)

Daniel Keyes, *Flowers for Algernon* (Harcourt, Brace & World, 1966)

T. S. Eliot. *Old Possum's Book of Practical Cats* (Faber & Faber, 1939)

Amy Bloom, *In Love* (Random House, 2022)

Anne Lamott, *Bird by Bird* (Random House, 1994)

Sarah Ruhl, the phrase "I can only imagine," *Smile: The Story of a Face* (Simon & Schuster, 2021)

"State Scorecard: State Medicaid Coverage Policy" report (LUNGevity, March 2020)

Thomas J. Roberts, MD, MBA; Aaron S. Kesselheim MD, JD; Jerry Arorn, MD, "Variation in Use of Lung Cancer Targeted Therapies Across State Medicaid Program," (*Journal of American Medical Association [JAMA] Network Journal*, January 2023)

Barbara Ehrenreich, "The Humanoid Stain" (*The Baffler*, 2019)

Mary Oliver, "Wild Geese," *Dream Work* (Random House, 1986)

Young Jean Lee, *We're Gonna Die* (Lincoln Center production, LCT3, 2021)

Aileen Kwun, "Why It's Time to Rethink Chinoiserie" (*Elle Decor*, May 2021)

Narjust Florez, MD, "Sexual Health Assessment in Women with Lung Cancer" (Shawl Study), (*American Cancer Society Journal*, 2023)

Peter Schjeldahl, on ways of seeing works of art over a lifetime, *The Art of Dying* (Abrams Press, 2024)

Jhumpa Lahiri, on thinking deeply on the transformation mythology in Ovid, *Translating Myself and Others* (Princeton University Press, 2022)

Stephanie McCarter, trans., *Metamorphosis* by Ovid (Penguin Classics, 2022)

Acknowledgments

So many kinds of kindness have made this book possible. If I have neglected to thank you here, let's blame it on medication-related brain fog. Emergency chocolate is always on the way to thank super-agent Lynn Johnston and her team, including Debbie Clayman at Lynn Johnston Literary. Thank you to the extraordinary team at Zibby Books, including Zibby Owens, Kathleen Harris, Anne Messitte, Diana Tramontano, Gabriela Capasso, Sherri Puzey, Jordan Blumetti, and Leigh Haber. I'm so grateful to be reunited with Elizabeth Shreve PR for this book.

Early readers: Neena Beber, Jenny Allen, Sarah Koskoff, Claudia Silver, Maggie Rowe, Jeanne Darst, Lisa Birnbach, Sandra Tsing Loh, and Moon Zappa. Deep thinking: David Ulin and Sarah Hochman. I wouldn't be here without: Hardye Moel and my family, Ezra Kahn, Lisa Gurwitch, Tom Sharpe, Maddy Rapp, Anne Hamburger, Rafe Jenney, Owen Jenney, Marc Turkel, Dashiell Beber-Turkel, Jessica Hecht, Adam Bernstein, Judith Newman, Jill Diamond, Jim Vallely, Heather Winters, Rose MacDowell, Tonya

Pinkins, Ali Wentworth, Madeleine Brand, Bart DeLorenzo, Sara Melson, Emily Lerner, Aimee Lee Ball, David Wallis, Helaine Olen, Susannah Blinkoff, James Lapine, DJ Paul, Denise Chamian, Judy Twersky, Cari Lynn, Gia Palladino and Michael Wise, Heidi Levitt, Marisa Silver, Caitlin Flanagan, Bill Maher, Juel Bestrop, Jake Mendel, Sally Turner, Barbara Wright, John Fleck and Randy LaBorde, Tanya Selvaratnum, Iris Bahr, Jeff Vespa, Michelle Kholos Brooks and Max Brooks, Sarah Norris, Cindy Chupack, Nicole Holofcener, Stephanie Black, Jodie Markell, Betsy Aidem, Sasha Emerson, Wendy Hammers, Larry Dean Harris and Strong Words, Larry Mantle, Scott Simon, Mandalit del Barco, Meghan Daum, Jean Hanff Korelitz, Susan Orlean, Jonah and Ellen Zimiles, Mitchell Kaplan, Richard Schechner for a lifetime of mentorship and lunch dates, Ruth and the Gurwitch Girls, Brenda Rippee, Jennifer Cunningham, Neil Weisberg and the friends and family rate. Cuteness suppliers: Eliana Fleisher, Maya and Amos Fleisher, Shirley and Betty. Thank you Eleanor and John Hammond. Thank you for walking with me, Jeremy Hammond.

Essential communities: Alissa Quart and the Economic Hardship Reporting Project. Suite 8 Writers, including Janelle Brown, Erica Rothschild. Invisible Institute West's Tom Zoellner, Wendy Paris and the Invisibles. Jamie Kabler and The Rancho Mirage Library. American Academy in Rome: Marla Stone, Gabriel Soare, Tiziana del Grosso, Aliza Wong, Laurie Anderson, Jhumpa Lahiri, Fabiana Ciccone, Judith Modrak, Satoko Motouji, and The Potluckers. Campfire: Maura Tierney, Katie Flahive, Dr. Nisha Sajnani, Alexandra Zaslav, David Hugo, Orlando Pabotoy, Susan Kaplan, Ily Huemer and Derek Sanders and La Esquina. Maximum Fun Network: Bikram Chatterji, Laura Swisher, and Laura House. CollegePath LA founders Jody Brooks and Susan Phillips, the Erma Bombeck Writers' Conference community, James Thurber House,

Jewish Book Council, *On Being Jewish Now* authors, H.O.D.G.—Hang Out Do Good, Maggie Wheeler and the Golden Bridge Choir.

Home teams: Dr. Paul Crane and Kathy Holland, Michelle Anderson, Dr. Ray Jalian, Dr. Raj Kanodia, Howard Flashberg, Judy Barrett, Harry Maring, and Dr. Shoshana Gerson. Teachers: Ashley Sharp, Georgia Junker, Steve Levitt, Mel Gottlieb, and Rich Panico. Tom Trellis and the Alcove Restaurant. Gratitude to Lauren Gibson and Tom Markley, Metropolitan Talent Agency. Discount Medical Pharmacy proprietors Sorin and Sona Kazangian.

One-of-a-kind agent and friend Bradley Glenn, Scott Kaufman, Natalie Lifson, Jordan Thompson, and Julia Buchwald for the years of dedicated representation.

Editors: Tara Parker-Pope, Jacob Brogan, Emma Allen, Honor Jones, Roberta Zeff, Kelly Horan, David Ulin, Maer Roshan, Samantha Dunn, Susan Brenneman, Lisa Hostein, Warren Bass, Susan Morrison. Teachers: Ashley Sharp, Steve Levitt, Rabbi Mel Gottlieb, Claudette Sutherland, and Rich Panico. Adam J. Fein and Drug Channels.

Dream team: Dr. Ravi Salgia, Razmig Babakian, Mindy Shirk, Antonieta Marquez, Shira Dingal, Luz Ramirez, Dr. Linda Bosserman, Dr. Joanne Mortimer. Thank you to surgeon and hugger Dr. Alice Chung.

Quality of Life Community: Kim Norris and Jim Baranski and team at LCFA, including Diane Mulligan, LUNGevity community, EGFR Resisters, Lung Cancer Research Foundation, WALCE, Arutha Kulasinghe, rockstar Lysa B., dearest pal Laura Book, the indefatigable Jill Feldman, sister in bitchiness Terri Conneran, Dusty Donaldson, Yvonne Diaz, Graham Hall, Emi Bosso, Janet Freeman-Daily, Dr. Sydney Barned, Lillian Leigh, Patti Saccenti and Paolo Capaccioni, Michel Itel and Lee-Anne Currie,

Dr. Upal Roy, Dr. Amy Moore, Lauren Machos, Josh Bergren, Dominique Stokes, Christine Clark, Maiyan Chau, Triparna Sen, Dr. Christine Lovly, Dr. Ross Camidge, Matt Smeltzer, Dr. Aakash Desai, Dr. Jacob Kaufman, Dr. Brendon Stiles, Dr. Stephen Liu, Dr. Narjust Florez, Dr. Jarushka Naidoo, Dr. David Carbone, Dr. Ray Osarogiagbon, Dr. Charles Rudin, Dr. Christian Rolfo, Dr. Jorge Gomez, Dr. Hitesh Batra, Dr. Silvia Novello, and Stefania Vallone. IASLC: Sara Lindsey, Barbara Bricalli, and the All Copays Count Coalition. The Communications Committee of IASLC.

Most important: Thank you to those of you who read the scans and scheduled the appointments whose names I never learned; the techs armed with warm blankets; phlebotomists whose patience I have tested; and Collier and the always friendly parking staff at City of Hope, Duarte.

About the Author

ANNABELLE GURWITCH is an actress, an activist, a two-time Thurber Prize finalist, and the *New York Times* bestselling author of six books. Her essays and satire have appeared in *The New Yorker*, *The New York Times*, *The Wall Street Journal*, and *The Washington Post*, among other publications. Her books include the *New York Times* bestseller *I See You Made an Effort* and *You're Leaving When?*, a *New York Times* Favorite Book for Healthy Living. Gurwitch cohosted the fan favorite *Dinner & a Movie* on TBS and was a regular commentator on NPR. She is a Jewish mother, lung cancer survivor and patient advocate, a terrible ukulele player, and an unrepentant cat lady who lives in Los Angeles.